DESIGN FUNDAMENTALS FOR THE DIGITAL AGE

LINDA HOLTZSCHUE AND EDWARD NORIEGA

A VNR book

JOHN WILEY & SONS, INC.

New York • Chichester • Weinheim • Brisbane • Singapore • Toronto

This publication is designed to provide accurate and authoritative information in regard to the subject matter covered. It is sold with the understanding that the publisher is not engaged in rendering professional services. If professional advice or other expert assistance is required, the services of a competent professional person should be sought.

Library of Congress Cataloging-in-Publication Data:

Holtzschue, Linda.
    Design fundamentals for the digital age / Linda Holtzschue
and Edward Noriega
        p.   cm.
    Includes index and bibliographical references..
    ISBN 0-471-28786-5

Printed in the United States of America

ACKNOWLEDGMENTS

Our thanks to Nino Mendolia, Alison Holtzschue and Charita Patamikakorn for their help in editing; to Esteban Vicente, Elizabeth Castagna, Ann Ledy, Lydia Johnston, Kevin Bubriski, Rick Noriega, Richard Day, Kingsley Parker, Michael Randazzo and Hae Young Yoon for their contributions to the illustrations. We are grateful to Donal Higgins and Jim Dixon, whose inspiration and encouragement lives on in our hearts and in this book.

And finally, special thanks to our families, especially Karl Holtzschue and David Baldwin, for their endless patience and support.

CONTENTS

PREFACE

If Leonardo Da Vinci were alive today, what platform would he be using?

This book is about the foundations of design as they have always been understood. The impact of the computer on design is addressed in that context. It is written for beginning artists and designers for whom the Digital Age is already in place.

It began as conversations between the authors, who found they were teaching identical courses on design fundamentals: one using the computer, the other using traditional media. One thought that "computer design" was an oxymoron. The other was tolerant of a fogy who hadn't even been to cyberspace.

A series of conversations began as a debate over the impact that digital design was having on students' ability to grasp the essentials of design. Was facility on the computer resulting in a lot of junk design, or was the computer freeing students from repetitive tasks and allowing them more time to address issues of visual thinking?

What started as fiercely opposite positions became a mutual education and, in the end, a shared conclusion: the computer is a natural step in design history. There is no difference between what Leonardo needed to know about design fundamentals and what a student today needs to know. Only the medium is new.

"The important thing to remember is that this is not a new form of life. It is just a new activity".[1]

---

[1] Dreifus, Claudia. "The Cyber-Maxims of Esther Dyson," *New York Times*, 7 July 1996, sec. 6, p. 19.

Chapter 1

ART AND DESIGN

**DESIGN FUNDAMENTALS / THE ARTS / BEAUTY / FINE ART / DESIGN /
TASTE / ART HISTORY, ART CRITICISM, AND AESTHETICS / VISUAL
COMMUNICATION / STYLE / INSPIRATION AND INFLUENCE**

"It's pretty, but is it art?"
Rudyard Kipling

Design Fundamentals

Design fundamentals are observations about visual experiences. Design fundamentals describe objective attributes of works of art and design like size, proportion, and color; they also describe how those attributes affect an observer. They are the foundation concepts used by artists and designers to construct and create. They make possible the analysis and criticism of works of art or design. They facilitate communication between teacher and student, critic and public. They are the underpinnings of visual thinking.

Design fundamentals are constant for two-dimensional images and three-dimensional objects, for static or moving images, for every medium, and for the art and design of every culture. Form, for example, is an objective quality. The words *star, triangle, rectangle, circle,* and *square* describe the physical fact of forms. Something is described as triangular or round as a matter of fact, not opinion. Forms can be assigned symbolic meaning, but in and of themselves they are objective figures and universally recognizable.

The concepts of design fundamentals can be organized in any number of ways—as two- and three-dimensional situations, as forms and their attributes like size and proportion, as different arrangements like symmetry or asymmetry, or as surface qualities. Design fundamentals are independent ideas only for purposes of study. Every work of art or design has a full range of visual attributes. No work of art or design consists of only one idea. The emphasis of one idea over others—color over form, or symmetry over movement, for example—gives each work its individual character. The emphasis of one idea over another is also where different aesthetic theories, which are *judgements* about what is beautiful or "correct" in art, diverge.

The Arts

The arts are areas of human creative effort that address nonscientific forms and ideas like painting, literature, philosophy, and music. In science a premise is tested repeatedly for consistency. If it can be demonstrated invariably to be true, like gravity, for example, it becomes scientific law. There's no real equivalent in the arts for scientific method. No premise can be proven in quite the same way.

Art is an umbrella term for an enormous field of human activities and products. It is first a general term for human skill. Magicians and physicians practice their art. Dickens's cleverest pickpocket was the Artful Dodger.

Art also means the tangible objects produced by human skill and the products of creative work and, finally, the use of imagination to make things of beauty.

Beauty

Beauty is the quality of an object or experience that gives pleasure to one or more of the senses. Sights, sounds, scents, or tactile sensations can be beautiful.[1] Natural beauty exists without

human intervention: it occurs outside of human control. Manmade beauty is a product of human effort. It can be a work of art, a symphony, an article of clothing, or a car. Whatever its end product, manmade beauty is a product of human skill and creativity (See Figure 1-1).

The association of beauty with virtue, or "goodness," is deeply rooted in Western culture. The Greek philosophers considered art and beauty to be separate concepts. Beauty concerned either the moral and good, or the mathematical, identified as geometry. Art was *mimesis*, the representation or imitation of nature. The

FIGURE 1-1.

A wooden walkway creates a frame for a Japanese water garden. The placement of plants and walkway are planned, but the beauty of light, shadow, and contrast of leaf forms are accidental effects of nature.

Fine Art

Greek premise that beauty and good are bound together persists in our unconscious. We still expect the princess in the fairy tale to be as good as she is beautiful. The beast, given the chance to show his true inner nature, emerges as a handsome prince.

When most people use the word *art* they are referring to the products of the **fine arts.** In Western cultures drawing, painting, sculpture, printmaking, ceramics, and sometimes architecture are traditionally considered to be the fine arts, but this short list is by no means universally acknowledged. In many cultures textile design, garden design, metalworking, and other disciplines are also considered to be fine arts, and new media are regularly proposed for inclusion in the category of fine art.

Restricting the idea of art to "things of beauty" excludes a great deal of creative work, including some masterpieces. The series of lithographs by Roualt that portray the Crucifixion of Christ do so with chilling power, but it would be hard to describe them as "beautiful." A definition of art must be elastic enough to accommodate a variety of works and ideas and specific enough to distinguish art from nonart in a reasonable way. One definition might be:

> *Art is something tangible and new created by human skill, the purpose of which is to communicate ideas and feelings using visual means. A work of art has the capacity to stand alone, conveying its message to the observer through the visual experience without a need for interpretation or reference to subject matter.*

A tangible work created by human skill, communicating an idea or feeling using visual means, and with the ability to stand alone can nevertheless be dull or mediocre. Great art is different. It leaps the barriers of time, place, sub-

FIGURE 1-2.
*The arts encompass
an enormous range of
two- and three-
dimensional disci-
plines including
(among others) sculp-
ture, painting, draw-
ing, architecture, and
digital art.*

ART AND DESIGN   5

ject, and aesthetic theories. Masterpieces have a unique quality perfectly characterized by Thomas Hoving as he saw for the first time an astonishing thirteenth-century painting:

> *"I stared at an enormous wooden panel, at least four feet square, entirely filled with the face of the young Virgin Mary, so translucent that I imagined a miraculous light had been illuminated behind it. No human face has ever been composed of such unlikely elements—a very long thin nose; an almost imperceptible mouth; a pair of giant soft black eyes, so large and penetrating they seemed to overwhelm all else. The features, taken separately, were bizarre, but together they bestowed upon the Virgin's face a reality transcending nature" (Hoving, 170).*

Great art can have no better definition than this: "a reality transcending nature" (See Figure 1-2).

The fine arts are categorized by their media. A *medium* (singular) is a material or substance used to produce a work of art like paint, clay, charcoal, metal, or stone. Buildings and sculptures require solid materials, although not necessarily rigid ones. Painters need colors that can be transferred from the artist's hand to a working surface. Prehistoric man drew with charcoal and colored earths, the tetrachrome palette of black, red, yellow, and white. A modern painter has available an almost infinite number of pigments and ways to mix them, but essentially painting has only advanced, not changed. A perfectly contemporary work still can be produced using prehistoric materials.

The twentieth century has produced the first wholly new medium since the prehistoric: electronic media, like television and computer monitors, produce images with light alone. The computer allows the artist to create and keep images made only of light. Technology has introduced a new way to produce art and a new way to see it.

Design

Art has been said to manifest *immanence,* a theological term meaning the attribute of being present throughout the universe. If art is universal, what makes one thing a work of art and a similar thing not? What is the difference between art and design? A painting and a sports car are products of creative work: each is new, each communicates an idea, each can be beautiful. How are they different?

Design also demands human skill, creativity, a tangible product, and the communication of ideas. Unlike art, design also implies utility. It involves an object for *use.* In a well-designed thing form does not just follow function; they are inseparable. "Beautifully designed" has a double meaning: pleasing to the senses and well-functioning (See Figure 1-3).

A *design* is a plan or model. An "original design" is a new and unique plan or model. Although a product prototype is made by a creative artist, the final product is manufactured by others.

Designed objects communicate their use. The message of a pot is "cook in me," a chair "sit on me." A car suggests comfort, speed, and safety. Poor design leads to poor function. The control panels of airliners are designed with great care. Good design can be the difference between life and death (See Figure 1-4).

Appreciation of good design may be the most intuitive and widespread form of art appreciation. A well-designed hammer will outsell equally serviceable but less-handsome alternatives.

Art and design are *categorized* by their media, not *defined* by them. The arts can accommodate

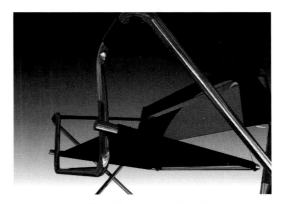

FIGURE 1-3. *A digital drawing of a Marcel Breuer chair demonstrates the skill of the illustrator as much as it does the art of the chair designer.*

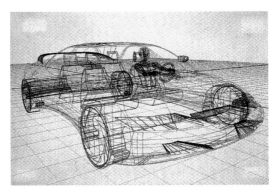

FIGURE 1-4. *The design of the car and the way it is drawn communicate its use; each is a visual metaphor for motion.*

new disciplines, new ideas, and new media. **The central experience of the visual arts is that they are means of communication.** The long-held distinctions between fine art and design, or between art and craft, have blurred. Many questions about art and design are answered best by the works themselves. Art is a visual language. It speaks to the viewer with open eyes and an open mind.

Taste

Art History, Art Criticism, and Aesthetics

Taste simply means preference, like a preference for vanilla over chocolate, jazz over opera, or Rembrandt over Andy Warhol. To say that someone has "good taste" infers that he or she has admirable (or "correct") standards for choosing one thing over another and, by extension, that some choices are intellectually and morally superior to others. "Bad taste" suggests moral and intellectual inferiority in the choice (and in the chooser). Taste, like concepts of beauty, has a strong cultural basis. Jack Lenor Larsen, writing about textiles, concludes that creativity and artistic preferences are, in great part, a response to the outside environment of the distant past. Larsen characterizes contemporary design preferences as a response to an increasingly mechanized and less-natural human environment (Larsen and Weeks, 5).

What is "tasteful" in one context (tattooing one's face, for example), may be considered appalling in another. To say that something is "tasteful" or "in good taste" bestows a seal of approval on the choice of one thing over another, but it says nothing about what the *reasons* for that choice may be. Some of those reasons are suggested in the field of study called *aesthetics*.

The world of art and design is an uneasy alliance of often combative groups: those who create art, those who study art, and those who criticize it. Design fundamentals provide a vocabulary for the evaluation of art and design.

Art history identifies and chronicles the lives and works of artists and movements in art and recounts their influences upon each other. Art history theoretically records without judgement, but like all histories it is contaminated by opinion. The most objective and original historian is subject to the influences of cultural context and time. A history of Medieval art written in the Renaissance will be considerably less admiring of that period than one written in the late nineteenth century.

Art (and design) criticism evaluates works of art and styles or movements in art. Criticism is the art of evaluating art. The usual way to critique a work is to judge it against prevailing contemporary standards. Popular art and design mirror the society in which they are created. They reflect current and acceptable taste. A second way in which art and design are judged is against new and innovative standards. To create a new style or to evaluate something against new standards challenges the social structure. The artist or designer who does so moves out of step with the time. The critic who applauds the new collaborates in promoting new standards of aesthetic "right and wrong." Each act is revolutionary, rejecting current standards and introducing new ones. Each act is also evolutionary: The history of art and design is an endless cycle of acceptance, change, rejection, and acceptance.

Aesthetics is the area of philosophy that is concerned with beauty and the doctrines (or principles) of taste, especially in the fine arts. Aesthetics is one of many intellectual disciplines that arose from the intellectual ferment of the Enlightenment. Aesthetics expanded and focused on the premise that beauty is a *standard* for excellence in works of art and that timeless, precise, and indisputable standards of beauty can be identified, ideals that establish for all time what is beautiful and what is not.[2] Aesthetics is a secular study that parallels a profound religious concept that perfection exists and, through human striving, can be attained.

Aesthetic principles are explicit statements about what constitutes beauty. They are judgements stated as truths. To say that "blue color is everlastingly appointed by the Deity to be a source of delight"[3] is to state an aesthetic principle. Architect Mies Van der Rohe, who rejected the forms and ornament of classical architecture, said that "Less is more" and helped to displace centuries of architectural tradition. Robert Venturi, an architect known for his exquisite attention to detail, has been credited with the retort—an alternative aesthetic principle—"Less is a bore."

Aesthetic principles use the vocabulary of design to describe the qualities of an ideal. They make it possible to evaluate works of art or design. It's impossible to assess the artistic merit of something without first characterizing exactly what is admirable about it and what is not.

It is a classic technique of propaganda to misrepresent political doctrine as aesthetic princi-ples. Soviet Socialist Realism depicted "heroic" workers engaged in "heroic" acts of physical labor; its aesthetic principles were based on entirely political concepts. The Soviet government officially rejected art works that did not meet state-instituted ideals (See Figure 1-5).

A more indirect example of politics determining aesthetic ideals is found in the neoclassical

FIGURE 1-5 *Soviet Socialist Realism— propaganda masquerading as poster art.*

ОТСТРОИМ НА СЛАВУ!

ВИКТОР ИВАНОВ

painting of the period of the French Revolution. Artists like Jacques Louis David (1746–1825) chose "democratic" subject matter from the ancient Greek and Roman histories and a rigidly austere style, rejecting in composition, colors, and subject the aristocratic and frivolous extravagance of the earlier painters Watteau (1684–1721) and David's own contemporary, Fragonard (1732–1806).

Aesthetic ideals can shift rapidly as a consequence of some revolutionary event or change slowly over time. The pace of change is irrelevant, but *change is inevitable*. Many works of art considered masterpieces today have been ignored or condemned in their own time. Matisse was called a "wild beast." The first performance of Igor Stravinsky's *The Rite of Spring* provoked a riot. The history of aesthetics is a history of standards against which things have been judged to be beautiful (or not) in some particular place and time. Ideals of beauty are transient.

For thousands of years before the advent of photography the arts afforded the only way to create a **pictorial** record. The subject matter in art, whether person, place, or event, was an area of primary focus. Prehistoric art probably meant to convey magic. Ancient art recorded myth and history. Medieval and Renaissance works of art were commissioned only by the very rich (and very few); almost invariably their documentary purpose was as important as the decorative one. Jan Van Eyck's *Arnolfini Marriage Portrait* (1434) was a legal document of its time. Public art was meant to inform and educate when few could read (See Figure 1-6). Church frescoes, paintings, and sculptures tell religious stories. Political messages for nonreading populations are also pictorial narratives: their storytelling power exemplified by Latin American political frescoes of the early twentieth century such as those of Diego Rivera.

FIGURE 1-6.
Storytelling at its best: Lancelot escapes a giant in this early narrative drawing from Le Roman De Lancelot Du Lac, c. fourteenth century, France.

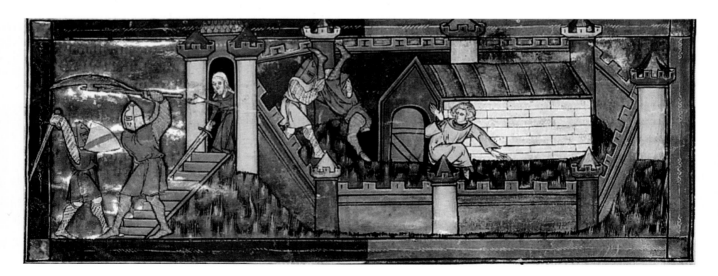

Style

Expressive content is the communication of feelings through visual means. Art and design are also vehicles for conveying emotion. There are visual cues, like strong contrast, intense color, and slashing diagonal lines, that impart dynamism and drama to a composition in a way that is independent of its subject. When emotionally charged subject matter is combined with visual excitement the communicative effect is breathtaking (See Figure 1-7). The stone Assyrian warriors now safely confined to the British Museum still have the power to terrify. Van Gogh's anguish whirls from his paintings. Edvard Munch's *Scream* can almost be "heard" with the eyes. Expressive content can also mean delight. The whimsical flying lovers of Marc Chagall entertain; the nudes of Renoir communicate joyful carnality.

Style is a kind of shorthand that describes a pattern or group of characteristics that are common to an object and others like it (See Figure 1-8). Styles generally take their names from the historic periods during which the works were produced or from intellectual movements of those periods.

Art Deco is an aesthetic movement of the early twentieth century. Highly stylized and deco-

FIGURE 1-8.
Style and humor in an English Regency "George Smith" chair, reproduced by Smith and Watson, New York, from an early-nineteenth century original.

Figure 1-7. Kaethe Kollwitz's woodcut War: The Widow *exemplifies the artist's ability to express a maximum of anguish with an austerity of line and form. (Location not indicated.)*

rative, it was inspired in part by the design forms of the machine. **Ming** is the period of Chinese dynastic ruling house (1368–1644); **Arts and Crafts** is a late nineteenth-century anti-Industrial Revolution political and aesthetic philosophy.

A lot of unspoken information is included in a phrase denoting style. Both country of origin and approximate date are implicit. A "Louis XV chair" has certain characteristics of scale, leg shape, wood used, carving, and finish, and was designed and fabricated during (or close to) the reign of King Louis XV of France (1715–74). A Louis XV-*style* chair, however, imitates design characteristics of the Louis XV period but has

been manufactured at a later date. No matter how skillfully made, a chair made in 1870 in the *style* of Louis XV is not a Louis XV chair.

The emphasis of one visual idea over others is also an important way in which aesthetic theories differ. In every style, one (or more) aspect of design is emphasized over others. That emphasis helps art historians determine the date and provenance (place of origin) of otherwise unidentified works. Fluid lines dominate the Art Nouveau style in France, color is soft and light/dark contrast is minimized. Art Nouveau works suggest lightness and line rather than heaviness or mass; they have a linear quality even in three-dimensional pieces (See Figure 1-9). Baroque art stresses dynamic movement and breaking out of two-dimensional space. Contrast of light and dark is typically pronounced. Based only on these visual indicators and without knowing the subject, age, or symbolism of a work, it's nevertheless possible to identify pieces from either period with reasonable accuracy.

Every era has a "signature"—a subtle emphasis of some elements over others—that is not evident in its own time. As time lends distance, that emphasis emerges. Well-made forgeries produced in one's own time can be difficult to detect, but fakes produced in another era are more easily identified because elements of style characteristic of the period in which the piece was made tend to surface in the fraud. A Louis XV-style chair manufactured in the nineteenth century may fool a nineteenth-century customer, but the stamp of the nineteenth century will probably be apparent to a present-day buyer.

Inspiration and Influence

An **inspiration** is something—a sudden thought, action, or realization—that induces a new idea or a new connection between ideas. Inspiration is a prompt for creativity in any field. The invention of the steam engine was as inspired as the "invention" of Impressionist painting. Inspiration isn't necessarily obvious or direct except to the "inspiree"—a mathematical equation may suddenly inspire a new way to paint.

An **influence** is an idea that has a modifying effect on other ideas. The single most influential force in early twentieth century design is probably the Bauhaus, a German school of art and design founded by architect Walter Gropius, which operated between 1919 and 1933. Bauhaus theories of design were cerebral, exacting, explicitly stated and came into being on the brink of the age of modern communication. These widely disseminated principles came to dominate European and American design in areas as diverse as industrial design and the fine arts.

The initial impact of digital design was to make enormous changes in the way design was *produced.* A parallel impact has been a change in the kinds of images that designers and consumers have come to expect. Digital imaging and the information superhighway have initiated an undercurrent of aesthetic change that is genuinely global. The "signature" of digital design is not yet fully formed. It is too soon to assess the exact nature and extent of its aesthetic impact, but that the impact exists is no surprise. The capabilities of any new medium—chalk, fresco, printing press, or light—have always influenced art, style, and design.

References

Hoving, Thomas. *King of the Confessors.* New York: Ballantine Books, 1981.

Larsen, Jack Lenor, and Jeanne Weeks. *Fabrics for Interiors.* New York: Van Nostrand Reinhold, 1975.

Endnotes

[1] The taste of foods is an exception; flavors are not generally thought of as "beautiful" or "ugly."

[2] Contemporary use of the word *aesthetic* has shifted from the original meaning; it is now used commonly, if inexactly, as a synonym for the word *artistic*.

[3] John Ruskin, Lectures on Architecture and Painting, 1853. In John Barlett, *Familiar Quotations* (Boston: Little, Brown and Company, 1980), p. 572.

Chapter 2

DIGITAL DESIGN

**Computer Anatomy / Storing Information / Hardware /
CD-ROM / The Monitor / Capturing Information /
Software / Platform / The Internet / Digital Design /
The Computer Medium**

"Now that we have the machines
let us, instead of imitating former products
and techniques, try to design goods that
are characteristic of machine production—
do not let us imitate former designs.
Let us, with the help of these technical
aids, produce the new."

Gregor Paulsson[1]

Computers have transformed the way we think, work, and communicate. Technology has taken us, in less than a generation, to a place where instant communication and information processing are ordinary events. The transition from the Industrial Age to the Information Age is complete. The computer has become the universal tool of the workplace.

The design industries have been at the center of this revolution. Computer skills are now a requirement for entry-level employment in almost every field. The computer has revolutionized the design industries in the same way that the printing press revolutionized the production of books. The printing press and the computer have a second parallel as well. A printing press cannot write and a computer cannot draw. Only the writer writes; and only the artist draws.

Every computer allows the user to store, sort, process (change), select, and retrieve information with astonishing speed. A computer has an "operating center," or "brain," called the **CPU** (Central Processing Unit). It has mechanisms for getting information in, storing it, retrieving it, a means of information output, and a short-term, working-in-only-memory feature called **RAM** (Random Access Memory). **Hardware** refers to the things that can be touched, like the computer and its accessories (monitor, keyboard, mouse, printer, etc.).

Software, programs, and applications are interchangeable names for sets of instructions that make it possible for the hardware to perform specific tasks. Software can't be seen or touched, but the user is aware of it as the statements, instructions, and graphics that appear on the monitor screen.

Every computer must have both hardware and software. Together they determine what kind of information can be stored and processed, how fast information can be processed, and the quality of the monitor display or printed page. There is an enormous selection of options in choosing hardware and software, and each choice affects the final output. No component is independent of the others.

Storing Information

Information (data) can be stored as analog information or as digital information. Computers store and process only *digital* information.

Analog information is continuous, like the information we receive from our senses. A wavelength of light, for example, is sensed as an unbroken stimulus. It can vary in intensity but it has no "breaks." An **analog medium** stores information in the same continuous way that it is experienced. There are no breaks in analog storage, just different points on a continuous curve. The thicker and thinner grooves of a phonograph record are analog storage (See Figure 2-1).

Digital information is information that is separated into discrete samples. Each sample is recorded and stored as a separate unit of information. Digital samples are so small that they cannot be understood individually. Retrieved information is understood as if it were continuous. A digital audio recording, for example, is sampled more than 44,000 times per second, and each sample is stored as a separate piece of digital information. Analog information cannot be used by a computer until it has been converted to digital form (See Figure 2-2).

Digital coding is the foundation of the computer's operating system. The smallest unit of coded information is a **bit.** A bit has only two options: on or off. Eight bits, grouped together, can be arranged in 256 different possible combinations of on/off. A collection of eight bits is a **byte.** A byte typically represents one piece of information—a letter, number, punctuation mark, tone, color, or something else—in the computer memory.

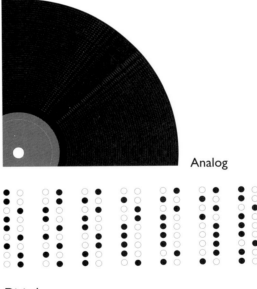

Analog

Digital

FIGURE 2-1. *Analog information is stored in the same way it is experienced: continuously like the grooves of a record. Digital data is saved as information broken into the smallest possible recorded "bits."*

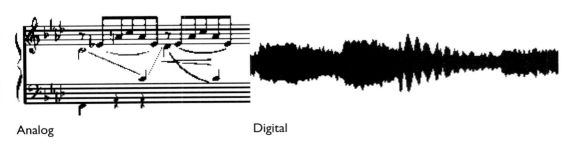

Analog

Digital

FIGURE 2-2. *Music is stored digitally as tiny fragments of recorded data.*

Hardware

A CPU contains one or more storage disks called hard drives. A **hard drive** is a rigid electromagnetic disk with a fixed capacity that determines how much information can be stored. A hard drive is both a storage system (or memory) for information and a means of retrieving it, like a record player and a record all in one (See Figure 2-3).

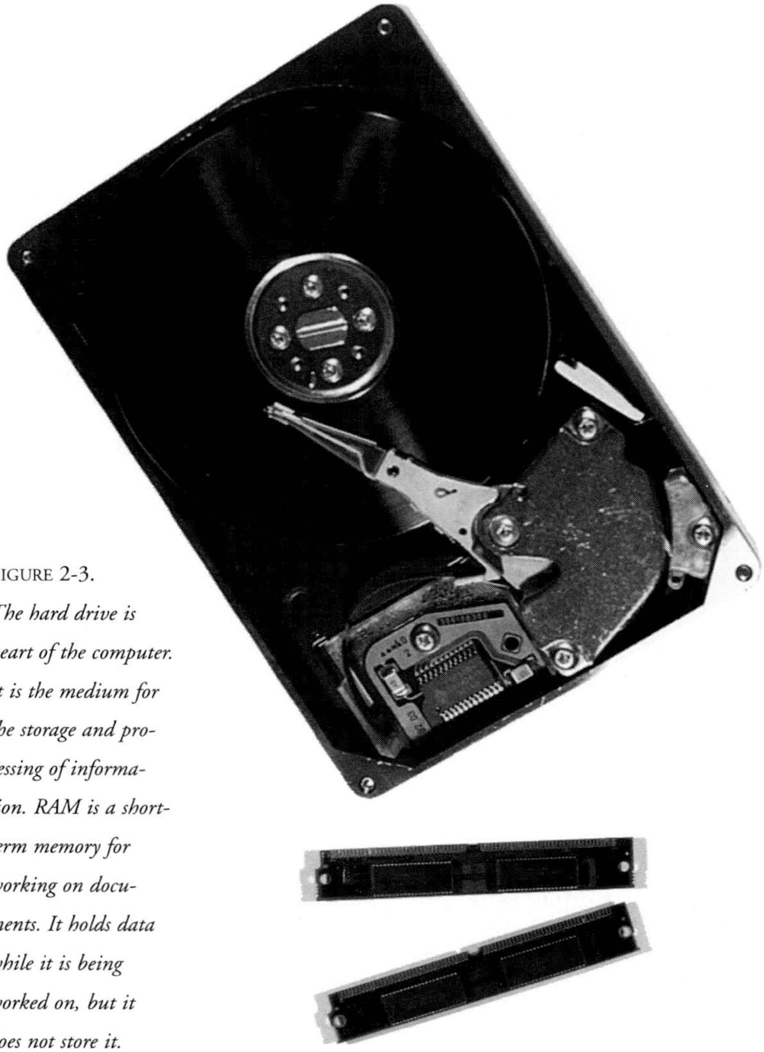

FIGURE 2-3.
The hard drive is heart of the computer. It is the medium for the storage and processing of information. RAM is a short-term memory for working on documents. It holds data while it is being worked on, but it does not store it.

The storage capacity of a hard drive is measured in bytes. The more bytes a hard drive has, the more information it can store. A kilobyte (K) is equal to 1024 bytes, a megabyte (MB, or meg) is 1024 K, and a gigabyte (GIG) is 1024 MB. The capacity of RAM is also determined in bytes. The capability of a computer to store and process information depends on the storage capacity of the hard drive and the work space available in RAM.

Programs become available to the user when they have been copied onto the computer's hard drive. Software operates when the user instructs the computer to copy the program from the hard drive, where it has been stored, to RAM. The user works in RAM, using the software to generate **documents** (for example, written text or drawings). When the documents are complete the user instructs the computer to save the documents (or not, as desired). Unsaved documents are erased from RAM and saved documents are copied to the hard drive. They remain stored on the hard drive until the next time they are needed. *Documents* that are created using software can be changed, but the *software* itself does not change. Users create and work on documents *within* the program.

Computers usually have one or more additional drives called floppy drives or disk drives. A **floppy drive** is a player that has no storage capacity. It allows the user to read and process information that is stored outside the computer on a removable, portable storage medium called a floppy disk, or **floppy.** The floppy is the "record" played by the floppy drive. Floppies

CD-ROM

have the advantage of being portable and are available with storage capacities ranging from 400 K to 1.2 MB. Floppies are slower in processing than other storage systems. There can be a noticeable delay between the user's input and the appearance of information on the screen.

A floppy is inserted into the **disk drive**, an opening in the computer. Work can be done directly on the floppy, or the stored information can be copied to the hard drive and worked on in RAM. Saved information can be returned to the floppy, to the hard drive, or to both for storage. Programs can be copied onto floppies from the hard drive and also the reverse—copied from floppies onto the hard drive.[2]

In addition to the hard drive and floppy drives, most computers come equipped with an additional drive called a **CD player** or **CD-ROM player** (or **CD-ROM drive**). CDs are **Compact Discs,** a portable storage medium. CDs are often used for music and sold as audio CDs (See Figure 2-4). Users need a device called a **CD-writer** (or **CD-burner**) to record information onto a CD.

Most of the compact discs used with computers are CD-ROMs. A **CD-ROM** is a removable, portable compact disc with a "read-only" format. Information on a CD-ROM cannot be added to, changed, or deleted. A CD-ROM has enormous storage capacity and can store multimedia information—text, sound, moving and still pictures. CD-ROMs are sturdy. Video images require a CD player (a floppy drive is too slow for moving pictures). Most CD-ROMs are **interactive:** Information is stored so that the reader can control the order in which it is retrieved. A CD-ROM looks just like an audio CD, in fact, audio

FIGURE 2-4. *CD-ROM is a portable medium capable of multimedia storage. It can store sound and video images as well as still ones and can allow the viewer to control the way information is retrieved.*

The Monitor

CDs can be played on the CD-ROM drive. Since CD-ROMs can store as much information as a good-sized hard drive, they are often used to store large programs like computer games and encyclopedias. At this time, the CD-ROM is the computer medium's closest counterpart to a book.

The **monitor** is the component with a screen. Images on the monitor screen are created by the distribution (pattern), strength (brightness), and colors of the light. The monitor screen display is the first and most immediate form of computer information output (See Figure 2-5).

The ability of a monitor to display detail and color is measured in two different ways. **Resolution,** the ability to display detail, is measured in pixels. The ability to display colors is measured as **bit-depth.**

A **pixel,** or "picture element," is the smallest unit of a monitor's screen display. The size of a pixel is measured as **dpi** (Dots Per Inch) on the screen. The "dot" represents a pixel. The more dots (pixels) per inch, the more detail that can be displayed and the higher the resolution. An average monitor has 72 dpi and will display reasonably continuous images. A screen with a lower dpi produces a ragged-edged image that is fragmented, like a mosaic. In addition to having different dpi, different monitors have pixels of different shapes. A pixel has a "footprint"—square or rectangular—so adjustments sometimes have to be made in drawing to accommodate them.

The number of colors that a monitor can display is determined by its bit depth.[3] Individual pixels can be altered in hue, value (light or dark), and saturation (vivid or dull quality). The number of ways in which a pixel can be altered is determined by its bit depth. Black-and-white monitors have a 1-bit depth. Each pixel has only two options, on or off, so the choices are black or white.

Figure 2-5.
Resolution depends on the monitor's dpi. Images with low dpi are blocky and fragmented.

Most monitors display colors and shades of gray. The human eye sees 256 levels of dark to light (a gray scale from black to white) as an unbroken gradation (See Figure 2-6). An 8-bit depth monitor (256 possible different combinations of on/off) can display shades of gray, which allows continuous shading, and 256 colors, a range adequate for most routine design tasks.

Bit depth tells only how many colors a monitor is capable of displaying. The software determines how many colors are actually displayed. The more colors the software has stored as coded information, the more memory (of a particular kind, video display memory) the computer needs

Figure 2-6.
The human eye perceives 256 steps of black to white as a continuous gradient of dark to light. Fewer than 256 steps are likely to be seen as separate steps.

to store and process that information. Monitors up to 36-bit depth, capable of displaying more than 17 million different colors, use powerful software that requires a tremendous amount of video display memory.

Other common means of output are **modems,** hardware that allows the computer to send and receive information through telephone lines, and **printers,** which transpose digital information onto printed pages.

A computer is useless without human input, or "data capture." The **keyboard** and **mouse** are the most familiar of a range of tools that allow the user to enter information into the computer for processing. A **stylus** allows the user to draw on a hard surface called a **tablet;** the drawing appears on the monitor screen. A **digital camera** captures images without film and uploads them into the computer. The images it captures appear on screen and can be manipulated and saved. **Scanners** take printed pages of drawings, text, or photographs, which start as analog information, and convert them to digital form so that the computer can process them. When a scanner is used in conjunction with OCR (Optical Character Recognition) software the scanned text becomes a document that can be edited in word processing. The resolution of scanners is also measured in dpi. Printed material is generally produced at a higher resolution (higher dpi) than screen images. Scanners range from a modest 300 dpi to commercial versions with thousands of dots per inch.

Software

Software brings the computer to life. Well-designed software is logical to use and takes advantage of the capabilities of the machine. Most people take advantage of only a fraction of a computer's capabilities, but good software encourages the user to venture further (Cotton and Oliver, 187). Software is task-specific. It allows the user to add, change, and delete documents only within the capabilities of the application. **Database software** uses sequences of instructions for information processing and selective retrieval. A database program can only process information that has been entered into it. **Design software** allows the user to produce new information. It uses algebraic formulas and graphs for problem-solving (Vince, 148).

Software controls how retrieved information is displayed on the monitor and how many colors will be available to the user. There are two kinds of display-screen programs for design software: pixel based[4] and vector-based.

Pixel-based software is used in **paint programs**. In **pixel-based software** the entire screen display—every pixel of every drawing—is held in memory. Elaborate drawings and simple ones require the same amount of storage. Editing a pixel-based image means that the computer must redraw the entire screen each time the user makes a change. Pixel-based software is slower than vector-based programs because it handles information in a different way. **Vector-based programs** store only a part of the screen display.

In pixel-based programs the resolution of the output is controlled by the software. Simple pixel-based programs use a standard resolution of 72 dpi on screen and print at that resolution. In an ordinary pixel-based program, what you see is what you get. More elaborate pixel-based software allows the user the option of saving and producing images from a range of dpi choices. Screen images are produced at 72 dpi and, if planned for use as screen images, are saved at that resolution. For printed images the user can select a higher dpi and save and print at that resolution.

Pixel-based images do not enlarge well. Enlargement means that the *size* of each pixel enlarges, not the overall *number* of pixels on the screen. As the size of each pixel increases, the number of dots per inch decreases. The decrease in dpi causes "jaggies," or stair-step edges in diagonal or curved lines (See Figure 2-7). The user can downplay the jaggies by **anti-aliasing**, a process of blurring a jagged line by adding a line of intermediate value between it and its background, but pixel-based software has inherent limitations in its ability to display smooth curves and diagonals.

vector-based

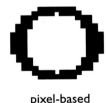
pixel-based

FIGURE 2-7.
Curves produced in vector-based draw programs enlarge well. Paint programs are pixel-based; curves become jagged when enlarged.

FIGURE 2-8. *A composition created in a pixel-based program. The artist emphasizes the attributes of the medium, using the pixels to create a fragmented image.*

Pixel-based programs display images as bitmaps. A **bitmap** is a image made up of pixels. The bitmap image on the monitor corresponds exactly to the information in memory (See Figure 2-8).

Draw programs for solid-object drawing use vector-based software. Images are generated by a mathematically plotted series of points[5] that appear as a screen display of lines or planes. The monitor repeats the lines or planes so quickly that no screen flicker is evident. A frequent use of vector-based software is to generate "wire-frame" drawings that depict three-dimensional forms as outlined edges without solid planes, as if they were models made of wire (See Figure 2-10).

Vector-based programs are very fast—only those pixels that are part of the drawing are saved, so less memory is necessary. Changes can be implemented quickly. The entire image does not have to be erased to rework a vector-based drawing.

Vector-based drawings can be enlarged without losing the sharpness of the image. The images produced by vector-based software are not controlled by the size of the pixel. Characters (letters, numbers) can be rescaled without losing resolution as they enlarge. Letters and numbers look good on the monitor in type of all sizes.

Vector-based software is device-independent. Because software does not determine the pixel size, the screen image can be produced at the highest resolution of the monitor. Vector-based programs also produce printed pages at a resolution determined by the *printer,* not at a resolution determined by the *software.* The extremely high-quality line that can be produced by a good printer makes vector-based software a natural choice for producing drawings that demand tight control (See Figure 2-9).

Both vector- and pixel-based applications include algebraic functions that allow actions like rotation, changes in scale, hidden line and surface removal, and changes in point of view. Changing one dimension in the drawing of a solid object alters the dimensions of other planes in ways that are not necessarily visible on screen. Programs for solid-object drawing respond to any change made in one view by automatically adjusting the dimensions of the whole (See Figure 2-10).

Applications can have both pixel- and vector-based functions. Most programs include computational features that protect designers against routine errors, freeing them to spend a greater proportion of time on aesthetic concerns than on technical ones.

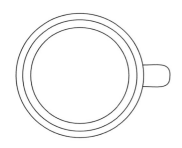

FIGURE 2-9. *Vector-based programs are an ideal venue for technical drawings, particularly in the execution of curved lines.*

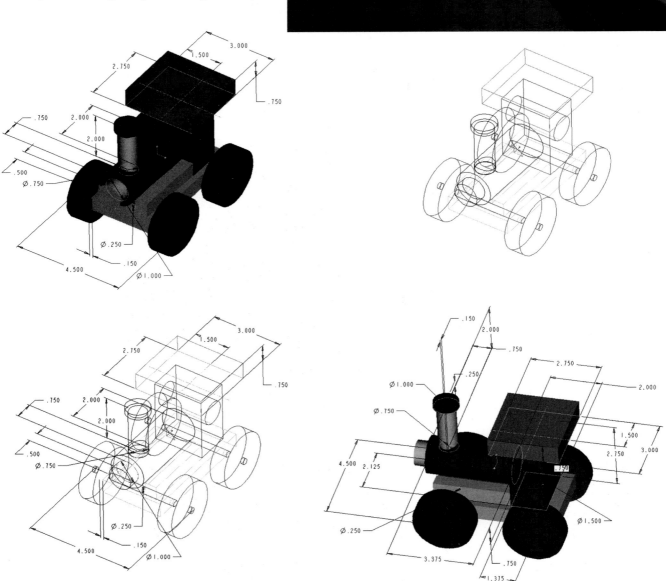

FIGURE 2-10. *The capabilities of digital drawing are apparent as the designer explores every possible aspect of a serious toy train, including a wireframe drawing.*

Platform

A **platform** is the combination of a particular type of computer and a particular operating system. There are a number of available platforms—Macintosh, PC, WindowsNT, UNIX, and others.[6] Each platform has features that enable it to perform certain tasks better than others. The platform plays the principal role in determining what software programs can be operated, because software programs are designed to operate on a specific platform and platforms are not always interchangeable. Macintosh, for example, is a platform that will not accept software designed for a PC. Some popular software is available in more than one version to serve individuals using different platforms.

The storage capacity of the hard drive and the work space available in RAM also play a part in determining what software can be operated. Each software program requires a certain amount of storage space on the hard drive and work space in RAM. A program will not run if it requires more storage or more RAM than a computer has available, even if software and platform are compatible. A computer with inadequate storage can often be upgraded by purchasing hardware that adds hard drive storage and RAM work space.

Users choose platforms, external storage devices, and amount of RAM that will operate the software closest to their needs. Most computers come with an operating system already installed and additional software can be purchased separately in the form of disks. The outside of the package tells the buyer what platform and how much memory is needed to run the program. Most commercial software is self-installing: the user inserts the first disk into the disk drive and receives instructions from it for installing the rest of the program.

The Internet

Cyberspace is an intangible reality of computer networks, telephones, television, satellite telecommunications links, and digital media. The **Internet,** or "Information Superhighway," is an emerging global source of mass communication in cyberspace. The Internet is a communications network, a means of linking remote computers. The Internet was developed originally by the United States Department of Defense in 1968 for emergency military communications.

The World Wide Web (WWW) or **Web** is a subset of the Internet. It is a source of accessible systems and databases via the Internet. Not all computers that are linked by the Internet are accessible through the Web. The Web was developed in 1989 to give scientists the opportunity to exchange information through the Internet. As computers proliferated, so did the use of the Internet and the Web.

Access to the Internet and Web is accomplished through **providers** like AOL (America Online) or MSN (Microsoft Network). Providers are the on-ramp to the Information Superhighway. A modem links each computer, through telephone lines, to the provider's communications network.

Information and communication are inseparable in cyberspace. Researchers have access to remote libraries. Commercial users advertise in the new medium of electronic marketing. There are "chat rooms" for any conceivable topic—individuals sign on to "chat" with each other by exchanging written messages.

Digital Design

Digital design is an umbrella term for design produced on a computer. The first digital design programs to appear were CAD (Computer-Aided Design) or CADD (Computer-Aided Design and Drafting), vector-based programs developed for architects and engineers. The original CAD programs were costly and required expensive and elaborate hardware. Similar programs, still out of reach for the ordinary consumer or small office, soon came into use for large-scale operations like textile manufacturers. Subsequent design software, both vector- and pixel-based, reached the general market quickly at lower cost and with more modest hardware requirements. Today both pixel- and vector-based CAD versions are available, and CAD is a basic tool of product design, architecture, and interior design offices. Pixel-based design programs of all kinds are used in thousands of offices (including nondesign offices) to produce brochures, leaflets, posters, and other printed material. Digital design is now available at costs within the reach of even the smallest firms.

The advantages of digital design to the design industries are straightforward: It reduces staffing needs, accelerates the design phase of product development, generates more consistently accurate production drawings, and introduces new means of product presentation through electronic marketing. Computers benefit the design industries directly by increasing the opportunities for exposure and profit.

The same capabilities that the computer offers to industry play completely different roles for designers. The nature of the computer itself is so different from any tool that has been available in the past that its advent has transformed the studio workplace.

The outstanding functional benefit of the computer to design professionals is its ability to generate multiple variations or views of a drawing with speed and facility. Computer drawing programs can make, on command, instantaneous changes in the shape, size, number, arrangement, and color of drawn images and patterns. Programs that "rotate" the on-screen drawing of an object made from one viewpoint so that it can be examined from other directions simulate walking around (or even through) the drawn object. Computers allow textile designers to consider endless possible color combinations, architects to study building proposals from every point of view, and graphic designers to explore different combinations of layout, type size, and face—all without the time, labor, and expense of redrawing. Virtually every design discipline makes use of the computer in some analogous way (See Figure 2-11).

The computer makes it time- and cost-effective for a single designer to perform work that in the past required support staff and, as a result, to retain more control over the outcome.[7] It's commonplace in large studios for a concept originated by a senior designer to be worked out in more detail by design or production subordinates. Architects, for example, employ draftsmen whose job it is to bring skill (but not creativity) to drawing their designs. The series of small choices that any drawing requires inevitably create a shift in some direction away from the original concept. Digital design promotes continuity by making it practical for a single designer to govern more closely the entire course of project development.

Computers have brought into the studio some functions that, although logically part of the design process, were in the past separated from it by technical necessity. Type is a major component in graphic design, often the principal design element. Graphic designers can now originate their own type designs, something unthinkable before computers, when type design was a separate art and styles were limited to about 50 faces. The computer has also made it possible to incorporate typesetting into design development. Until the advent of computers typesetting was performed outside the studio—and away from the artist's critical eye—by a professional typesetter.

Digital design makes it realistic for individuals and small firms to compete against larger firms for projects that would once have been impossible for them to produce. The computer has given the purchasers of design more choices and the sellers of design a larger market. It has made the design playing field wider and more level.

Designers have global access to fresh ideas through the Internet and the Web, which serve as forums for the exchange of information and professional networking.

Perhaps the most important consequence of the computer revolution has been its liberating impact on the studio environment. Any design project is a problem that has to be solved within a deadline period. Because so many alternatives can now be examined in the same time that once allowed consideration of only a few, adventurous solutions can be explored without risk, cost, or penalty. Digital design helps to foster an atmosphere in which bold and innovative thinking can flourish.

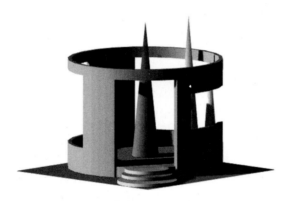

FIGURE 2-11. *Draw programs that produce solid-object drawing include perspective, shadows, and highlights for a maximum effect of three dimensions.*

Most users approach the computer as a tool that expedites the design process. It's true that the computer is a design tool (or a whole toolbox, or even a whole staff), because it has the capacity to perform so many different tasks. Whatever the computer is—tool, instrument, device, or machine—it is also, by any standard or definition, a *medium* with attributes that have no equivalent in the past. The image on the monitor screen can be both a means and an end: a way to compose and the actual design product.

An artist's medium is something that translates one visual reality into another, like a landscape into a painting; or something imagined into visualization, like the *idea* of a dragon into a *model* of a dragon. A medium is experienced first by the artist as a means of creating something, then as an end when work is finished and it remains a physical part of the design product. A tree drawn with a crayon becomes a crayon drawing.

Computer drawing and painting are forms of computer input. The artist working with a computer literally draws with light. Digital images are characteristically flat, because texture requires that the medium have substance and light does not. Light can be displayed as "broken" into small areas to dapple a surface, but it cannot have actual texture. A digital drawing appears on a screen that is remote from the hand creating it, so eye–hand coordination is different from conventional drawing.[8] Screen drawing remains transient, fluid, mutable—alive to change until it has been printed or saved.

Printed material is one kind of computer output. It is also a *category* of visual communication.

Design programs are used most often for the preparation of material that will be printed. The computer is superbly suited to these tasks, from the rendering of architectural plans and graphic designs to landscape plans, textile designs, and a multitude of other uses. Printed material produced from computer drawing is experienced visually in exactly the same way as printed material prepared using any other medium—pen, pencil, marker, paint, or anything else.

Monitor screen images are also a form of visual communication and computer output. *The screen image is an alternative to the printed page. Like printed pages, screen images can be saved, stored, and circulated to different readers.* A completed work for the monitor screen can be stored on a floppy disk or CD-ROM and distributed through disk sales, **e-mail** (electronic mail), as a planned event on the Internet, Web, or television. Unlike printed material, screen images can be interactive, allowing the viewer to select information in any order, and sound can be included to enhance the visual experience.

The visual impact of screen images is very different from that of printed pages. The light of a screen has a brilliance unlike paper and ink. Drawings that include motion are lively; they demand the viewer's attention in an active way. Some moving images are so successful in conveying an impression of depth that they are thought of as three dimensional even though they lie unmistakably on a two-dimensional plane.[9] Screen images that include motion occurring over time are developing as a new design category: time-based art.[10]

Using the computer to prepare material for printing employs only part of the computer's potential. Screen images that are the design product make full use of the medium. Digital design is not an alternative to traditional media like pencils or paint. It has its own validity. Digital design is a new vehicle for the actualization of design ideas, a new kind of visual experience, a new application—a new and different kind of design reality.

Inevitably, computers will store and process information in new and faster ways. Software will have capabilities not yet imagined. Imaging will be refined. Screens will be manufactured with increasingly fine resolution—even holographic images are on the horizon. In the world of computers the phrase "current technology" is practically an oxymoron. Advances in technology do not change the attributes of the medium. The capabilities of hardware and software will alter and advance, but the essential nature of the computer medium—of light, motion, and time—exists now.

The creative potential of the computer is only beginning to be realized. The challenge of digital design is not to find ways to perform new technical tricks; it is to create a new imagery that reflects the new medium. The generation of artists and designers who meet this challenge will do so in a surprisingly traditional way. Digital design requires only those things that good design has always demanded: skill in use of the medium, a mastery of foundation design concepts, and innovative thinking. Only the writer writes; only the artist draws.

References

Endnotes

Cotton, Bob, and Richard Oliver. 1994. *The Cyberspace Lexicon.* London: Phaidon, 1994.

Vince, John. *The Language of Computer Graphics.* London: Architecture Design and Technology Press, 1990.

[1] Paul Greenhalgh, *Quotations and Sources on Design and the Decorative Arts,* (Manchester: Manchester Press, 1993), p. 72. Gregor Paulsson in *Design and Machinery,* 1919.

[2] Software is purchased on disks and is intended for use only by the purchaser. Copying of programs that are protected by copyright laws, called piracy, is illegal.

[3] Bit depth does not mean actual depth. It is a word used to quantify a monitor's color display capability.

[4] Pixel-based images are also called **raster images.**

[5] See Chapter 4, section on World Coordinate Space page 65.

[6] According to Peter H. Lewis, "Apple's Best Hope: On-Line Sales," *New York Times* 13 August 1996, Section C, Page 5, computers will be on the market shortly that allow the user to select the platform (operating system) of choice. They will no longer be confined to one platform or maker.

[7] Support staff is not team design. Team design is a collective effort that occurs when a group of designers, often headed by a leader, works together to solve a problem.

[8] The left-side-of-the-brain function in drawing is a subject much explored; how remote drawing fits into this function is unexplored and potentially very interesting.

[9] See Movement Parallax, Chapter 6, page 114.

[10] The technology of computer, television, and movie images is increasingly analogous. The monitor image is discussed here as a design medium only.

Chapter 3

EYE AND MIND

**SENSE AND EXPERIENCE / SENSATION AND STIMULUS / THE NERVOUS
SYSTEM / SYNAESTHESIA / PERCEPTION / SYMBOL AND CULTURE /
VISION: LOOKING AT THE LIGHT / VISION AND IMAGE / VISION AND
COLOR / ADDITIVE COLOR / SUBTRACTIVE COLOR / INFLUENCES ON
COLOR PERCEPTION / THRESHOLD / INTERVALS AND GRADIENTS /
MORPHING / VISUAL FIELD AND CONE OF VISION / MOVING IMAGES /
FORM, LINE, AND FIGURE-GROUND SEPARATION / GESTALT
PSYCHOLOGY / ART AND DESIGN**

The eye is not satisfied with seeing.
Proverbs 1:8

Sense and Experience

The senses connect us to the world. They bring to us the experience of sight, sound, smell, taste, and touch. The senses are our first defense against injury and primary guide to sustaining life. Warmth attracts, but heat prompts withdrawal. Thunder threatens and music gives pleasure. Things that give pleasure to the senses are said to be beautiful and things that offend the senses are ugly. We are drawn to light and pull away from darkness (See Figure 3-1).

Vision is first in the hierarchy of the senses—nearly 80 percent of our perceptions are visual. Sight is crucial to our ability to navigate in the environment. It is so primary to understanding the world that words about sensory experiences, like "beautiful" or "ugly," unless they are otherwise defined, are assumed to be describing something seen.

A sensory occurrence alone—a touch, taste, smell, sight, or sound—is an incomplete event. Perception is the understanding and awareness to what has been sensed. Experiences, even "sensory" experiences, are really a fusion of sensation and perception.

Art and design are visual *arts,* but they are not exclusively visual *experiences.* That the experience of art and design includes the sense of touch is acknowledged by museum signs that ask PLEASE DO NOT TOUCH. The feel of silk, or wool, or a manmade fiber is part of the "experience" of a textile. There are other, odder, sensory reinforcements of visual experience in the arts. Thomas Hoving tells of a connoisseur who asserted (but evidently could not demonstrate) that he could establish the authenticity of a bronze by its smell, and of a scholar who could (and did) accurately date ancient brickwork by tasting the mortar (Hoving, 32).

Physiology studies the body and its functioning. **Psychology** studies behavior, or how organisms react when they are stimulated in different ways. Physiology and psychology together have produced a great many theories about how human beings sense and understand the world, and much of this study has been focused on visual perception.

Theories about *how* we see translate directly into studio techniques that create impressions—of size, space and depth, movement, and direction—and that prompt recognition and emotional response. The designer who understands the fundamentals of human perception understands how to direct (and sometimes even control) the way a design outcome is perceived.

FIGURE 3-1.
*The senses—sight,
taste, hearing, touch,
and smell.*

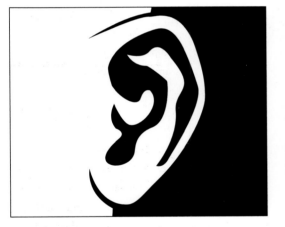

Sensation and Stimulus

A **sensation** is the purely physical experience of sight, sound, smell, touch, or taste. Sensations are provoked by a **stimulus,** something that the body encounters from the environment. A stimulus can be chemical, experienced as smell or taste; pressure, experienced as touch or hearing (pressure against the eardrum); or light, experienced as sight. The strength of a stimulus can be measured: The amount of light emitted by a light source is measurable, as is the amount of pressure exerted by one object on another.

The ability to detect a stimulus is sensory **acuity,** or *sharpness.* Sensory acuity is a measure of the weakest stimulus a person can detect, like a faint sound or image. Acuity also determines the point at which an individual can no longer discriminate differences between two similar things, like the difference between similar colors, musical notes, or perfumes (See Figure 3-2).

Individuals vary to some extent in their ability to hear, see, taste, smell, or touch because of differences in physiology, health, and age, but human acuity for all the senses has known limits. "Silent" whistles for dogs produce a sound that is outside the limit of human hearing. There is light that some animals and insects can see but that no human being sees because it is outside the range of human vision.

FIGURE 3-2. *One way to measure acuity is as a measure of the smallest difference that can be sensed between two close stimuli. Some people can see the differences between very close grays; others need more distance between samples in order to see differences.*

The Nervous System

The **nervous system** is the human body's communications pathway from the outside world to the brain. It is made up of three kinds of cells: receptor, transmitter, and brain cells. Receptor cells receive information from the outside world (stimuli) and change it into a form of electrical energy that the brain can use.[1] Transmitter cells carry these signals to the brain, which identifies each signal and tells the body how to react.

The brain decodes a sensory signal first by identifying which sense has been stimulated. Each sense sends electrical signals that are characteristic of the stimulus that triggered them. Signals from each sense are received by the brain in a separate, specific location. Damage to one of these locations will damage (or cause the loss of) that sense. For example, if the brain is damaged in the area that identifies stimuli originating from the sense of smell, the sense of smell will be altered or lost.

The brain identifies which sense has been stimulated, then discriminates specific qualities within that sense. In music, for example, it discriminates between notes; in smell, between roses and lilacs; in vision, red from blue.[2]

Taste, touch, and smell require a direct contact with a stimulus. Sight and hearing receive stimuli more indirectly. Hearing receptor cells receive waves of pressure (sound). Vision occurs when receptor cells in the eye detect light. Sight and hearing are sometimes called the "higher senses," although it's not clear whether this is because they receive stimuli more indirectly than the other senses or because they are associated with the "higher" cultural expressions of music and art.

Synaesthesia

Synaesthesia is a long-recognized but largely unexplained phenomenon in which one sense responds directly to the stimulation of another. There are reports of blind persons, as well as sighted ones, who are able to determine the colors of objects through touch.[3] A woman reports a humming sound when she enters a certain red room; the sound stops as soon as she leaves the room. A man reports a strong taste of lemon when he listens to a particular piece of music.

Recent research indicates that the sensory pathways to the brain are connected to each other in ways that can be demonstrated but are not yet understood. The idea that there undiscovered connections between the senses seems less surprising when we remember what an ordinary thing it is to experience chills—a reaction of the skin to change in temperature—from an emotional, musical, or visual experience.

Perception

Perception is the definitive connection between human beings and their environment. It is the brain's response to sensation. Perception is cognitive, or "knowing": it identifies, or "knows," what has been sensed. Perception is not measurable; it can only be described. Perception adds understanding to the sensory experience and supports and reinforces the life-sustaining functions of the senses. Perception also acts as a filter, separating out useful information from the sensory overload of everyday life—traffic, neon lights, boom boxes, multimedia advertisements, sirens, thunder, street signs, television, etc. (See Figure 3-3).

Perception is learned from a mixture of direct experience and cultural teaching. **Recognition,** the ability to identify a sensation, is the first step in perception. Recognition develops for all the senses with astonishing rapidity, beginning almost at birth. By adulthood human beings have acquired and stored an immense "library" of recognized sensations. New sensations, unless they are accompanied by additional information, are identified by referring to this stored information. A new sensation is recognized, correctly or incorrectly, by associating it with a familiar one that has similar characteristics.

FIGURE 3-3.
Sensory overload was an aesthetic ideal for Ludwig II of Bavaria. No wall or ceiling of his palace (built 1897–81) is flat; every surface is covered with ornamentation.

Symbol and Culture

Culture is the social structure that establishes what is important to a particular group of people. It determines to a great extent how objects and events are perceived and what responses must be made to them. In the 1981 movie *The Gods Must Be Crazy,* a Coca-Cola bottle tossed from an airplane is thought by Aborigines to be a heavensent sacred object. Its arrival sets off a series of misadventures because two cultures—the European and the Aboriginal—interpret the same objects and events in completely different ways.

Cultures and their institutions establish the meanings of symbols. A **symbol** is something that represents something else. Symbols link two previously unconnected things, usually a visual image and an idea. Symbols are specific to their cultures: red lights mean "stop" in most of the world; in China they mean "go." A phonetic letter is a symbol that represents a sound, but the *H* in the Cyrillic alphabet represents the sound "*en*" (See Figure 3-4). A corporate logo is a simple image that stands for a complex organization. The Coca-Cola script logo is said to be the world's most recognized symbol, but no symbol is truly universal. A symbol has meaning only when that meaning has been learned (See Figure 3-5).

FIGURE 3-4.
Even familiar symbols have different meanings in different contexts. The letter "H" represents the sound "aitch" in the Roman alphabet and the sound "en" in the Cyrillic alphabet.

FIGURE 3-5.
Some symbols strive for universal meaning. Recycling is suggested in this way.

Most people experience any given sensation in much the same way. The sense of sight is universal—a triangle is never sensed as a circle. Perceptions, however (what does the triangle *mean*?), are modified by culture, gender, age, health, education, social or economic status, and countless other factors. These external forces influence what individuals conclude about any sensory experience—what they perceive—and how they react to it.

The world is understood by the senses and the mind together. The word *perception* can also be used to mean the sensory and cognitive experiences together. *Perception,* from this point on, is used in that collective sense—to mean the complete experience of sensing and understanding information from the world outside the body.

Vision is the sense that detects the environment through the eyes, organs that are specialized to receive light. Light and vision are inseparable. People who believe they can see in the dark can't really do so; they are simply able to detect a very faint stimulus. No one can see in the complete absence of light.

Light is visible electrical energy. Light is emitted by light sources: naturally occurring ones, like the sun or firelight, or manmade sources, like incandescent, fluorescent, or halogen lamps,[4] or television or computer monitors.

Light sources emit energy in regular pulses or waves, like ocean waves. The waves are emitted at different distances apart, called **frequencies.** The distance between each peak of emission is **wavelength.** Wavelengths of light are measured in nanometers (nm). The human eye is able to sense wavelengths of light from about 380 nm to about 720 nm.

Wavelengths of visible light that are emitted at specific frequencies are seen as individual colors. The colors of visible light range from red—the longest wavelength—through orange, yellow, green, blue, and indigo (blue-violet) to violet, the shortest wavelength. The seven-hue **spectrum** of science, or spectrum of physics, is the full range of visible colors of light.[5]

Vision and Image

Red, green, and blue are the **primary colors of light.** New colors result when one light primary is mixed with another. The red and green wavelengths combine to make yellow light. The blue and red wavelengths combine to make magenta (red-violet) light, and the blue and green wavelengths combine to make cyan (blue-green) light. Yellow, magenta, and cyan are the **secondary colors of light.** When all three light primaries are combined they form white (or colorless) light. The red, green, and blue wavelengths must be present for light to be white (See Figure C-4A).

Sources that emit white light are called **general light sources.** Most general light sources emit all wavelengths (colors) of the visible spectrum, not just the red, blue, and green.

Isaac Newton first demonstrated the color-component nature of white light in the late seventeenth century. He passed white light through a prism, which refracts ("bends") light in such a way that each of its component wavelengths emerges separately as an individual color (See Figure 3-6). A rainbow is an example of a natural prism: Tiny water droplets in the atmosphere act as prisms and split sunlight into component colors.

Light enters the eye through an opening at the front called the *pupil* and falls on the inside back of the eye, called the *retina.* The **amount** and **pattern** of light falling on the retina creates an image that is carried from the retina to the optic nerve, then along the optic nerve to the brain, where there it is identified (See Figure 3-7).

FIGURE 3-6. *When white light is passed through a prism, the wavelengths are bent (refracted) and separate into individual colors.*

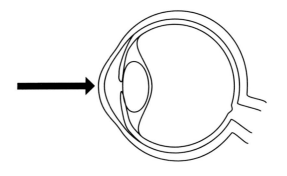

FIGURE 3-7. *Light entering the eye through the pupil passes directly back to the retina, the area at the back of the eye. Images and colors are transmitted from the retina to the optic nerve, then to the brain.*

EYE AND MIND   41

An object is seen when light reflected from its surface creates a pattern of light and dark on the retina. Objects can't be *seen* without light, but their reality can be *experienced* through other senses, like touch, taste, or smell.

Images on the retina can also be generated by light alone, without an object. Screen images are patterns of direct light emitted by a monitor. An image generated by direct light cannot be verified by other senses. It is transient, existing only as light, and when the light is turned off the image ceases to exist.[6]

Colors are seen when only one or a few specific wavelengths of light reach the eye. An object has substance that can be sensed in other ways, but color does not. Color is light alone, whether it reaches the retina as direct light or as reflection from a surface. In the absence of light color does not exist (See Figure 3-8).[7]

The retina is made up of two kinds of light-sensitive receptor cells, **rods** and **cones.** Both are connected to the optic nerve. The rods and cones respond selectively to available light. Cones dominate vision when a great deal of light is present. Cones are responsible for color vision and for the ability to see detail. Objects appear more colorful and fine detail, like small print, is clearer when cones are dominant. Rods dominate vision in lower light. Rods are responsible for peripheral—surrounding, less focused—vision. Colors appear muted or grayed and fine detail is more difficult to see when rods are dominant.

The fovea, a tiny area at the back of the eye, contains only cones. The rest of the retina contains a mixture of rods and cones. Standard eye examinations that eye charts use measure visual acuity as the ability to see detail, essentially measuring the detail aspect of foveal (cone) vision without measuring color vision. The separate tests for color vision are administered much less frequently.

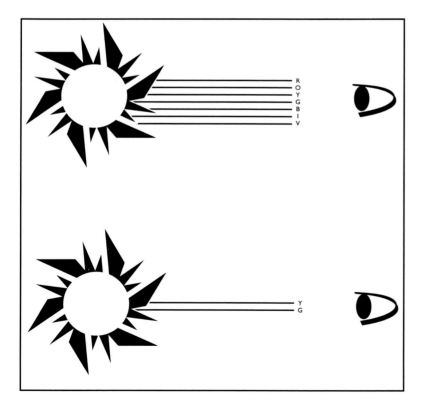

FIGURE 3-8. *Most light sources emit all or most of the wavelengths of visible light, and that light is perceived as white. When only one or a few wavelengths are emitted, the light is seen as a color. Colors seen as direct light (including the light from monitor screens) are additive colors.*

Additive Color

Subtractive Color

The illuminant mode of vision occurs when only two variables are present: a viewer and a light source. The viewer sees images and color as direct light.[8] Colors of light are **additive colors** or **additive mixtures.** The red or green of traffic lights, the colors of neon signs, and the images of color television and computer monitors are familiar examples of additive color. (See Figure C-4A).

An average person is able to see about 150 distinctly different colors, or steps between wavelengths, of light. These steps are differences in hue, like steps between red and orange or between blue and green. This number does not include darker, lighter, or more muted (grayer, duller) variations of each hue. The 150 visible colors and their darker, lighter, and duller variations mean that most individuals can discriminate millions of variations in colors.[9]

Monitor screens are light sources. The inside of a monitor screen is coated with light-emitting materials called *phosphors.* The phosphors are bombarded with electrical energy and react by emitting light. Screens range from 1-bit-depth monitors that display only white light (producing only black-and-white images) to 36-bit-depth versions that can display more than 17 million separate colors. The images and colors that appear on a monitor screen are direct light. Monitor images and colors occur in the illuminant mode of vision, and the colors seen on a monitor screen are additive mixtures.

The object mode of vision has three variables: a light source, a viewer, and an object or surface. Light reaches an object or surface and reflects, or bounces, off it and that reflected light reaches the eye. Until the advent of television and computers, colors and images were rarely seen as direct light. Nearly everything was seen as light reflected off objects and surfaces in the environment.

The tangible world is made up of matter, or materials. One property of materials is that they modify light. They do so in three ways:

A material absorbs *light, soaking it up like a sponge so it is lost as visible.*

A material transmits *light, allowing it to pass through, like light passing through glass.*

A material reflects *light. Light reaching the material bounces off it, changing direction and scattering. Some or all of the reflected light reaches the eye.*

Transparent materials transmit the light reaching them.[10] Transparent materials do not create a barrier to vision. Objects on the far side of a transparent material are visible. **Opaque** materials absorb or reflect all the light that reaches them. An opaque material does not allow any light to pass through. **Translucent** materials transmit some of the light reaching them and absorb the rest; the total amount of light that passes through them is changed. A translucent material can transmit so little light that a viewer cannot discriminate forms on the other side, or it can transmit enough light (and shadow) that

FIGURE 3-9.

*Transparent material
(a) allows light to
pass through it.
Opaque material (b)
either absorbs or
reflects the light
reaching it.
Translucent material
(c) allows a part of
all wavelengths to
pass through it and
the total amount of
light that reaches the
other side is reduced.
Filters (d) allow one
or a few wavelengths
to pass through and
absorb the other
wavelengths.*

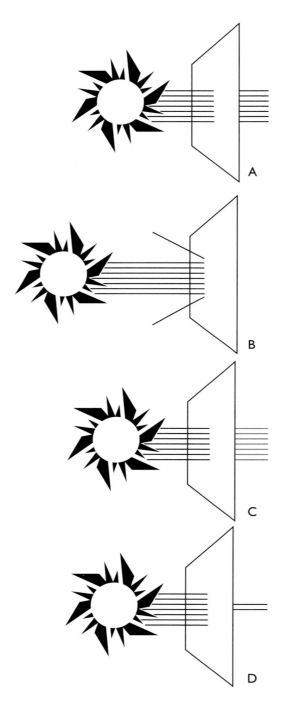

forms on the other side are obscured but still visible. Many textiles are translucent, as are materials like frosted glass (See Figure 3-9).

Color is seen in objects when a special kind of material called a **colorant** is present (See Figure 3-10). A colorant modifies light selectively. It reflects only one or a few wavelengths (colors) of light reaching it and absorbs the rest, so they are lost as visible. Colorants can be applied to an object, like dyes or paints, or they can be an inherent part of a material, like the chlorophyll in green leaves.

When light from a general light source reaches an object with a white colorant, all wavelengths of the light are reflected. The object has light reflectance but no apparent color—it is seen as white. White light reaching an object with a black colorant is almost entirely absorbed. That object will appear black, and equally colorless.

When white light reaches an object with a green colorant, all (or most) of the wavelengths are absorbed except the green. The green is reflected back to the eye, and the object is perceived to be green. An object with a red colorant reflects only the red wavelength and appears to be red, and so on (See Figure 3-10).

Colorants can only reflect a wavelength that is already present in the light source. If a light source lacks a particular wavelength, that color cannot be seen in objects under its illumination.

Not all light sources are white. The sodium lights that are common on highways, for example, emit almost entirely yellow light. Because they emit little or no red wavelength any red colorants, like those in lipstick or the red lines on road maps, appear black under sodium illumination.

Colorants do not reflect and absorb light perfectly. A colorant may absorb some of a wavelength and reflect some of it, or reflect two or three (or more) wavelengths at the same time. The number of possible combinations of reflected wavelengths combined with the average person's ability to see about 150 different colors and their darker, lighter, and duller variations make the number of visible colors nearly infinite.

The colors of objects and surfaces are called **subtractive mixtures** (or **subtractive colors**). Subtractive colors are seen by reflected light. The colorant selectively "subtracts" (absorbs) some of the wavelengths reaching it; remaining wavelengths are reflected and reach the eye as color (See Figure C-4B).

The mechanisms of the human eye for sensing light are the same whether the light reaches it directly from a light source or indirectly as reflection from an object. It is still true that most images and colors are seen as subtractive mixtures—light reflected from the world around us—but more and more hours, both work and recreational, are spent at monitors, looking directly at light.

FIGURE 3-10. *Wavelengths of white light reaching a colorant are selectively absorbed and reflected. The absorbed wavelengths are lost as visible. Reflected ones reach the eye and are seen as color. Color seen as reflected light is subtractive color.*

Influences on Color Perception

Threshold

The perception of color in objects is modified by unconscious expectations. **Memory color** is a kind of expectation about familiar objects. What is assumed or remembered about the color of an object—the "orange" of an orange, for example—influences observation. Many observers will "see" a preconceived idea about color even if the reality is substantially different.

Color constancy means that the eye and brain adapt to all general light sources as if they were the same. Familiar objects and locations retain their color identity under different conditions. The same colors seen in daylight and at night under incandescent light may appear dramatically different, but the mind's image overrides what is actually seen.

Groups of close colors will be perceived as identical whether or not this is actually the case. In an all-white kitchen the whites of the refrigerator, counters, cabinets, and the ceiling paint may all be somewhat different, but the immediate and cumulative effect will be that they are the same.

The **threshold** of vision is the point at which an individual can just detect a faint image or a faint light. Threshold is also measured as the point at which a person can just distinguish between close samples, like the smallest difference that can be seen between two close grays or very similar reds.

The world operates on the premise that there is something called "normal" vision. Threshold is different for each individual, but it is a very small difference. Common sense tells us that people see essentially the same images and colors (although their perceptions of what they have seen may vary).

Clean, crisp monitor images depend on a pixel size that is below the threshold of vision. Pixels must be small enough that the normal eye cannot detect them as separate elements. The smaller the pixel, the sharper the screen resolution.

Design of signage, furnishings, books, architecture or interiors, pamphlets, instrument panels, or anything else is done on the assumption that small individual differences in normal vision are unimportant. A designer chooses letter style and size for billboards or the phone book, or colors for packaging, on the assumption that everyone will see the design outcome in just about the same way. Designing for special groups like the elderly or visually impaired, or for special circumstances like areas of hazard, requires special sensitivity and attention to visual concerns, but it is rare for *individual* differences in threshold to drive the design process.

Intervals and Gradients

An **interval** is a step of change between visual sensations. Intervals can be progressive steps of change from dark to light, or between colors, or steps of change in shape, size, or some other quality. Intervals can also occur between repetitive elements that alternate, like a series of voids and solids or a pattern of stripes (See Figure 3-11).

Intervals are perceived as a series of separate steps whether those steps are very close together, very far apart, or somewhere in between. Intervals can occur on a two-dimensional surface or in three-dimensional space. Nonvisual intervals also have a place in digital design. Intervals occur between sounds and over time.[11]

A **gradient** is a series of progressive intervals that displays a gradual increase or decrease of some visual quality like lightness, color, or texture (Arnheim, 275–80). A gradient is a blending. Gradients are made up of intervals so close that individual steps cannot be discriminated. The intervals of a gradient are below the threshold of vision. Shading—a "wash" of color from dark to light, or from one hue to another—is a gradient (See Figure 3-12).

Gradients are visually powerful because they are perceived collectively as a single idea. Both intervals and gradients can be used to create an impression of distance and depth on a two-dimensional plane, or to direct focus by leading the eye from dark to light. Gradients create an impression of roundness or volume on a flat surface. A gradient that is interrupted by an irregular section loses its coherence as a single image.

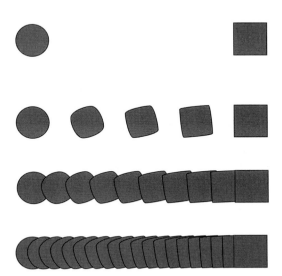

FIGURE 3-11. *Intervals are visible steps of change in some quality like color, lightness, or form, like these intervals from round to square. Intervals can be spaced far apart or close together.*

FIGURE 3-12. *Gradients are changes that occur too gradually for steps to be seen separately. Each change is below the threshold of vision.*

The same is true for regular, progressive series of intervals—the series, not its steps, is the whole. A series of progressive intervals that is broken by an irregular step also loses its force because the larger idea is degraded (broken) into smaller and less-important parts.

Morphing is a computer image-processing technique that uses intervals to change one image gradually into another (from *metamorphosis: meta* = change, *morph* = body). The artist begins with two images: a start and an end. Common points are designated on the two images. The points will relate to each other as the image changes. The number of frames (steps) required for transition is selected, and the software takes over the transition—the images melt into each other in a series of steps (See Figure 3-13). The magical effect of morphing is available as software to designers, but morphing has probably had its greatest impact on the entertainment industry (Cotton, 134).

FIGURE 3-13.
Morphing is a digital image-processing technique that changes one image into another in a user-selected number of steps.

Visual Field, Cone of Vision, and Line of Sight

A **visual field** is the extent of area that can be seen by the two eyes of a viewer standing in one position. Human beings have a visual field about 90 degrees from center left or right, a visual field that is about 180 degrees horizontally.[12] Left–right eye movement is more spontaneous and has a greater range than up/down movement. The vertical field is about 65 degrees up or down, a range of 130 degrees (See Figure 3-14).

The fovea is at the center of the visual field. The acute sharpness of foveal vision extends only one or two degrees from center. Images become progressively less clear as objects move away from the center of the visual field. For this reason most things are not seen completely and clearly in one single visual "bite." Looking at anything involves constant eye movements, called *saccades,* that allow the fovea to move across and around the contours of the object being studied (Solso, 23–25).

The tiny portion of the fovea that is in the sharpest focus is the center of the line of sight. The **line of sight** is an imaginary line from the center of the eye (the foveal center) to a point of focus, a view straight ahead. The **cone of vision** is the angle of vision that is in good focus, about 22–30 degrees each side of the line of sight, or 45–60 degrees overall. The cone of vision is considerably narrower than the whole visual field and affords a concentrated focus. It also provides a visual comfort range; images in the cone of vision require a minimum of "searching." Most drawings are confined to the cone of vision. The

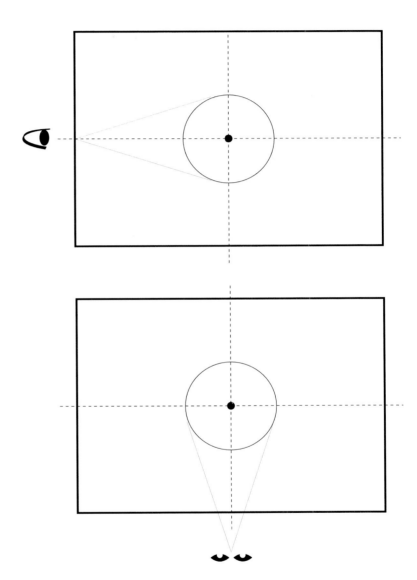

FIGURE 3-14. *The human visual field is wider than it is high. A viewer standing still in one position can see about 180 degrees left and right and about 130 degrees up and down. The cone of vision is an area in good focus that is about 22–30 degrees in all directions from the center at the center of the visual field, or about 45–60 degrees overall. The line of sight at the center of vision is a narrow area of acute focus no more that two or three degrees from center.*

concentrated focus of a monitor image is a natural result of that screen size and placement relative to the user; both factors place it well within the cone of vision.

Moving images depend on a series of progressive still pictures that change more rapidly than the eye can follow. **Persistence of vision** occurs when these progressive images are perceived as continuous motion. A light that is flashed on and off approximately 50 times per second is seen as steady brightness. In television and on videocassettes, progressive images are separated into two sets of alternating parallel lines. Each set of images changes every 25 to 30 seconds, so the screen is never blank and the resulting 50 to 60 changes per second are perceived as natural, continuous motion. (Cotton and Oliver, 161).

Form, Line, and Figure-Ground Separation

A form is the essential shape of an object or figure. **Form** is an arrangement of parts that differentiates one thing from another—like a fish from an kangaroo—but without individual identity.

A form is recognized first as something distinct from the background, a perceptual event called **figure-ground separation.** Forms become visible when the eye can segregate areas because there is dark/light contrast between them. Dark/light contrast is essential to form perception. Forms that exist in physical fact become invisible without it: An igloo remains a tangible reality in a blizzard, but it can't be seen.[13]

The continuous points where forms adjoin appear as an *edge.* An edge defines the contour, or outline, of each form. The edges of forms are experienced visually as **lines.** Lines that are drawn on a page or screen are really elongated masses with little width: ultra-skinny forms. Like everything else, a line is visible only when there is a dark/light contrast between it and its background. Black line drawn on black paper can't be seen.

An old cliché states that "there is no line in nature." It is true that there is no "thing" that is a line between two forms. But if line is not a *physical* reality, it is a *perceptual* reality. The edges of forms are perceived as lines, literally as "out"-lines (See Figure 3-15).

An aspect of vision called **lateral inhibition** increases the eye's ability to distinguish edges. When a pattern of light and dark contrast reaches the retina, the cells that receive the light part of the image inhibit the ability of the ones next to them to detect light. As a result, areas next to bright spots appear darker. The greater the quantity of light, the more lateral inhibition takes place: Light areas appear lighter and dark areas appear darker. Lateral inhibition helps make it possible to "read" forms whose contours are degraded (broken or incomplete) by emphasizing their edges.

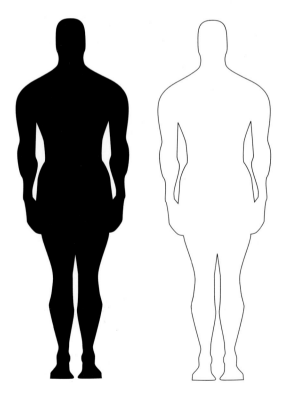

FIGURE 3-15.
Figures are recognized as whole and separate from their background. The edges of figures are perceived as outlines, or lines.

Gestalt Psychology

Gestalt psychology is a branch of psychology that suggests that pattern and recognition are essentially inseparable in form perception. Gestalt theory attempts to explain why it is possible to understand and identify forms even when they are partial, fractured, or fragmented images. It theorizes that things are perceived by *pattern*, not by the single stimulus, and that we see as much—or more—with the mind as we do with the eyes.

The central idea of Gestalt organization, called the "Law of Simplicity,"[14] states that *every stimulus pattern is seen in such a way that the resulting structure is as simple as possible.* The law of simplicity means that the brain groups small stimuli and merges them into the simplest possible larger idea. Dotted lines drawn in a circle are understood as a circle, not as a series of tiny arcs. Word games like crossword puzzles are verbal illustrations of Gestalt theory. The incomplete "words" d-g and c-t are immediately recognized as most likely to represent *dog* and *cat*.

Other Gestalt laws about organization are extensions of the law of simplicity. They state that similar things appear to be grouped together; that things that are near to each other appear to be grouped together; that connected points in straight or smoothly curving lines tend to be seen as belonging together; and that lines tend to be seen as following the smoothest path (See Figures 3-16 and 3-17).

Our instinctive perception of incomplete forms as whole forms is not paralleled by design software. The mind sees a partial outline as a completed figure and understands the whole form as a single area, or mass. Software fills only the area between two points, so an incomplete outline is filled as separated masses, not as a single whole.

The need to establish pattern from chaotic information suggests that some kind of order is essential to understanding. Everyday evidence tells us that the human mind is always trying to

FIGURE 3-16. *Smoothly curving lines that follow a continuous path are understood to be connected even when they are interrupted by open space. The figures they define are understood as whole forms, not fragmented ones.*

FIGURE 3-17. *Gestalt theory explains why a line of separate flags is seen as a line, not as individual flags.*

Art and Design

create order out of apparently disconnected bits of information. The "urge to order" expresses itself in the organization of information into categories: good, bad, indifferent, or animal, vegetable, mineral; into levels of importance; A, B, C, or 1, 2, 3; into progressions of size, weight, quantity, price, and/or color. Gestalt laws do not explain form perception completely or perfectly, but they do reinforce the idea that disconnected information is most easily understood as part of a larger and more structured whole.

Art and design are visual experiences that exist on multiple levels of understanding. There is an immediate impact that is almost wholly sensory. At first glance something is pleasing or it is not. It enables an American to think of a carpet from Turkestan as beautiful, a Frenchman to admire a bronze head from Benin, a Japanese to be enthralled by a Vermeer painting. Immediate impact is universal in design.

Works of art and design can be symbolic. Symbolism is recognized only by viewers for whom that symbol is familiar, but others, unaware of the artist's meaning, may identify personal (and equally valid) symbolic meanings.

Finally, art and design are communications. Advertisements say "want me, buy me." The communicative power of works of art and design is wildly variable. Some works transcend language and culture, others do not.

The sum of these factors determines a viewer's ultimate response to any work. That response is modified by all the factors that affect sensations and perceptions: physiology, culture, gender, education, age. *An artist controls the design process, but the final perception of the outcome belongs to the viewer. It can never be fully predicted or controlled.*

References

Arnheim, Rudolf. *Art and Visual Perception.* Berkeley and Los Angeles: University of California Press, 1954.

Cotton, Bob and Richard Oliver. *The Cyberspace Lexicon.* London: Phaidon, 1994.

Hoving, Thomas. *King of the Confessors.* New York: Ballantine Books, 1981.

Solso, Robert L. *Cognition and the Visual Arts.* Cambridge, Massachusetts: The MIT Press, 1994.

Endnotes

[1] The process by which receptor cells transform energy from the stimulus to a form of electrical energy that the brain can understand is called **transduction.**

[2] E. Bruce Goldstein, *Sensation and Perception* (Belmont, California: Wadsworth Publishing Company, 1984), p. 135. There are several theories about how the brain does this. One suggests that there are specific nerve fibers for each sensation; another that the brain identifies "red" or "blue" by identifying some pattern in the impulses received. Goldstein suggests that both theories have validity and are in force.

[3] A possible explanation for this may arise from an ability to detect wavelengths and differences between them through touch. Individuals with a deficit in one or more of the senses tend to develop greater acuity in the remaining ones. Once told that a certain tactile sensation means "red," a person with that sensitivity would be able to distinguish repeatedly the "red" sensation from others.

[4] *Lamp* is the correct term for a light bulb.

[5] The spectrum of light is the spectrum of science. Its number of colors and primary and secondary colors are different from those of the artist's spectrum. There are many different spectrums for various disciplines in science and art. See Chapter 7.

[6] Movie screen images are slightly different, created by projected colors of light that are reflected from a white screen. They are also transient light images.

[7] Color can exist without vision because it can be measured by scientific instruments without anyone seeing it; a sort of parallel to "if a tree falls in the forest and no one hears it, is there a sound?."

[8] Infrared, the longer wavelength beyond red, and ultraviolet, the shorter wavelength beyond violet, are visible to some animals and insects but are outside the human range. These wavelengths can be made visible with special optical equipment.

DESIGN FUNDAMENTALS FOR THE DIGITAL AGE

[9] Goldstein, *Sensation and Perception,* pp. 132–33. Color-deficit vision is rare. Only about one person in 100,000 sees no color at all. About 1 percent of the male population and less than .02 percent of the female population suffer from some form of partial color vision loss.

[10] Some light is always lost as it passes through a material, so strictly speaking a transparent material allows almost all of the light reaching it to pass through.

[11] The **single interval** is the point at which an individual can just tell the difference between two close samples, or the point at which a detectable interval cannot be inserted between two very similar things. The single interval is determined by an individual's threshold. Like threshold, the single interval is slightly different for each person and has little importance in design.

[12] See also **Golden Section,** in Proportion, Chapter 4, p. 76.

[13] Figure-ground ambiguity is a frequent device in design. Reversible figure-ground images range from simple vase/profiles outline examples to the complex, exotic, and progressive figure-ground reversal images of traditional Indonesian batik fabrics or the disorienting works of artist M.C. Escher.

[14] Also called the "Law of Pragnanz." *Pragnanz,* loosely translated from the German, means "good figure."

Chapter 4

POINT, LINE, AND PLANE

DESIGN PROCESS AND DESIGN CONCEPT / COMPOSITION / POINT / LINE / PLANE / PICTORIAL SPACE / WORLD COORDINATE SPACE / DRAWING / FORM AND SHAPE / ABSTRACTION / PURE FORM / SIZE / SCALE / PROPORTION

"Art attempts to find in the Universe, in matter as well as in the facts of life, what is fundamental, enduring, essential."

Saul Bellow[1]

Design Process and Design Concept

Design process (or creative process) is problem-solving. It is what designers "do." Design process is initiated by a problem, moves through creative thinking and design development, and ends in a design solution—a product. A **design concept** is a solution that addresses the broad issues of a design problem without resolving specific details.

A good design concept responds equally to practical issues and aesthetic ones. It creates a framework for design development. Exploring the consequences of a variety of design concepts is a time-consuming part of the design process. A fatal criticism of any design solution is that it is "a big idea, not well worked out." The computer does not change a single requirement of the design process, but it does expedite it. Design, like genius, is "one percent inspiration and ninety-nine percent perspiration."[2] The computer reduces the perspiration.

Composition

A **composition** is something meant to be sensed as a whole. A composition is the outcome of the design process. It is a planned arrangement of separate elements like lines, forms, and colors that together make up a new and distinctive single entity (See Figure 4-1). Composition also means the act of arranging design elements: it is both an *action* and a *result*. In every composition some elements are emphasized over others, but each contributes to the impact of the whole. A composition is greater than the sum of its parts.

FIGURE 4-1. *Mixed-media composition in ink, acrylic, and string on paper.*

Point

A **point** is the place where composition begins. A point is a location in space. A point has no size, no shape, and covers no area. It indicates position alone, whether that position is on a two-dimensional plane or in three-dimensional space. Something is needed to indicate a location that covers no area, so points are usually represented by a small mark or dot.

Most people think of a dot as "being" a point, but it is not. A dot makes a perfectly good point for the purposes of drawing, but the distinction between a point and its "dot indicator" is a real one. There are essential points in design (and particularly in digital design) that are never marked.

Implied points occur when some arrangement of lines or forms directs the eye to an unmarked, but definite, location. When two lines intersect, the place where they cross each other is a point (See Figure 4-2). A **focal point** is a location of emphasis in a composition. Most focal points are implied points, not marked ones.

The "point" of something is the heart of its meaning. "To point" is a way to direct attention. A "point of view" is the position from which something is seen (whether that position is in physical or intellectual space). Compositions, two- or three-dimensional, have starting points, ending points, and focal points. Points in design are about "where."

Digital design demands a heightened awareness of points. In addition to their key functions in visual thinking, points are the hidden structure of drawing software. Digital compositions can include motion, so another kind of

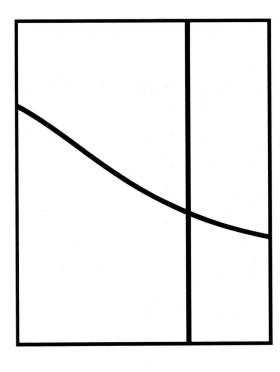

FIGURE 4-2.
Implied points occur at every place where two lines intersect, creating focus in compositions.

unmarked point—a point in time—becomes an element of composition. Music or spoken words can be integral to the "wholeness" of a digital composition. Time and sound are planned in the same way as lines, forms, and colors.

Composition embraces every element that is sensed as a part of a whole. It is an inclusive process.

Line

A **line** is a series of connected points in a single plane and in a single dimension. Lines begin and end at points. The direction of a line from one point to another is its **extension** or **path.**

A line is about action. It is a "moving dot" that leads the eye along its length. If a point says "where," a line says "how"—it indicates the path to get there. *First and foremost, lines communicate direction* (See Figure 4-3).

A drawn line is a directional mass with length but no (i.e., very little) width. Drawn lines are **actual lines.** A drawn line can curve or be straight, move in one direction or change direction, be continuous or interrupted, or plunge off

a page. An **open-path line** begins and ends at different points (See Figure 4-4). It divides space without enclosing it. A **closed-path line** starts and ends at the same point. It rejoins itself to enclose space (See Figure 4-5).

A **broken line** is a drawn line that is interrupted at intervals. A broken line is understood as continuous because of Gestalt laws—A directional series of small lines is perceived as a single simpler one. The dots or dashes of a broken line do not have to be closely or evenly spaced. A line that maintains its direction will be understood as continuous even if it has substantial gaps (See Figure 4-6).

FIGURE 4-3.
Three similar compositions with strong vertical lines; each composition pulls the eye upward.

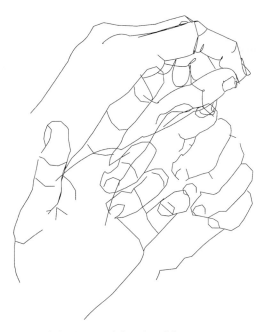

FIGURE 4-4. *Open-path line digital drawing suggests hands without enclosing space.*

FIGURE 4-5. *Closed-path lines rejoin to enclose space in this digital drawing. Lines in drawings done on the computer must connect from point to point in order for the form to be filled.*

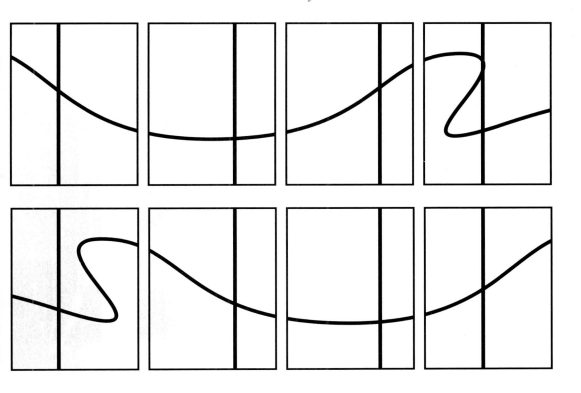

FIGURE 4-6.
Lines that are drawn in a continuous direction appear to be connected even when they have breaks.

An **implied line** occurs when a group of similar things is arranged in a directional way. People waiting outside a movie are perceived first as a line and only later (if ever) as individuals. Implied line exists without being drawn. It too illustrates Gestalt theory—similar things arranged in a directional way lose their separate identities and are seen as a larger idea.[3]

Line is probably the most versatile tool available to the designer. It can be a visual shorthand,

Line quality is the way a line is made: its hard or soft edges, its weight, its uniform or varying thickness. The expressive power of a drawing can be more a result of its line quality than of its subject.

Hard lines are crisp and clean edged. The drawings they produce are clean, controlled delineations. **Soft lines** are blurred, fuzzy, rough, or raggedy along their edges. They merge into the background rather than contrasting sharply

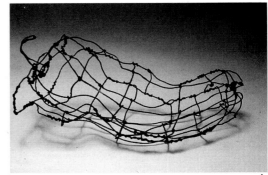

A

B

FIGURE 4-7.
Lines grouped together can give an impression of mass or roundness. Kaethe Kollwitz's The Weavers March.

conveying the impression of a form by the economical device of tracing its contours. Lines separate forms from their background. They enclose or divide pictorial space. Lines can be clustered to give an impression of mass or grouped in different densities to suggest roundness (See Figure 4-7). Line is characteristic of two-dimensional art and design but not exclusive to it. Wire sculptures use line to delineate solids and voids in space (See Figure 4-8).

FIGURE 4-8. *Wire sculptures use line to delineate solid and void in three-dimensional space. (a) is a wire sculpture; (b) two drawings of it.*

FIGURE 4-9. *Soft lines communicate a soft form in this traditional figure drawing.*

FIGURE 4-10. *A digital drawing exercise in line weight.*

FIGURE 4-11.
Line that varies in thickness appears to turn in space.

Plane

with it. Soft line suggests depth (See Figure 4-9). Jack Lenor Larsen calls the fragmented surfaces of nature a source of "psychic relief" from the manmade environment (Larsen and Weeks, 10). Soft lines also offer the psychic relief of unplanned variation.

Line weight is the width or thickness of a line. Light-weight lines are thinner and heavy-weight lines are thicker (See Figure 4-10). **Even lines** are uniform in weight. **Uneven lines** vary in weight. They have a lively, accidental effect. They give an impression of turning in space and contribute depth and movement to flat surfaces (See Figure 4-11).

The variations possible in line—in weight, edge, and direction—are infinite. The choice of one kind of line over another for a drawing is a decision about what will best illustrate an image or idea.

A **plane** is a two-dimensional surface that has two fixed dimensions, length and width, and a single direction in space. A plane is flat. It has area (a measurable surface) but no depth. *On a plane, every point shares the surface.*

A **picture plane** is a flat drawing field—a canvas, a display screen, a piece of paper, or any other plane that holds (or can hold) an image on its surface.

A **ground** is an actual material on which design elements—lines, forms, and colors—are laid. A piece of paper or textile is a ground. Ground has substance and texture. The picture plane of the screen display is an intangible display of light, a drawing field without substance.

Pictorial Space

World Coordinate Space

A picture plane is a blank wall. It stops the eye at its surface and at its borders. Images disrupt the surface of a plane, and that disruption translates into **pictorial space.** *Pictorial space is a sensed extension of the picture plane into depth.* Flat forms are interpreted as lying "on" the picture plane. Drawings of solid objects or environments are understood as reaching into picture plane, as having foreground and background.

Pictorial space is a premise that helps artists and designers communicate three-dimensional ideas on a picture plane. It involves some mental accommodation—a willing suspension of disbelief. Pictorial space is a drawing field that infers three-dimensional attributes to two-dimensional space. Pictorial space is never mistaken for actual depth. The world exists outside its edges.

World coordinate space[4] describes the mathematical basis of the drawing software that makes up the monitor's pictorial space. It does not describe the pictorial space of a monitor as it is *experienced by the user.* The monitor screen appears as a window that opens into space. The frame of the window is floating—it can be repositioned, so space extends not only forward and back, but also left and right and up and down. The world exists not outside the monitor, but inside it, and the drawing field is potentially infinite in height, width, and depth.

Cyberspace is a term coined by William Gibson to describe the movement of information and images in a chartless electronic universe. It is a new reality so hard to grasp that Gibson calls working in it "consensual hallucination" (Cotton and Oliver, 54).

Software is a vehicle for the exploration of cyberspace. Absolute fact (the earth is round) and what we experience (it seems flat) do not always coincide. One is *factually* valid, the other is *functionally* valid. Software is capable of creating an illusion of depth so convincing that it is easier to understand screen drawings as three-dimensional than as the two-dimensional figures they really are. The user and the observer accept that the *act of drawing is taking place in three-dimensional space and that the finished drawing exists in three-dimensional space.* Each is a willing participant in "consensual hallucination." We believe what we see. Three-dimensional drawing is a perceptual reality.

Drawing

Drawing is the translation of an objective reality or an idea into a linear representation. Whatever else it may include, drawing begins with line.[5]

Drawn lines are made by a hand moving a tool across a surface. In traditional drawing the tool moves directly on the picture plane. In digital drawing the hand guides a remote cursor across a screen. Traditional drawings develop directly on the surface of the picture plane. Digital drawing is indirect. It is either saved as a screen image or transposed to paper by a printer. *Traditional drawing and digital drawing are activities so different that they can be considered different skills; in fact, almost as different activities.*

All lines are drawn from point to point. Pixel-based programs employ two axes that lie on screen at right angles to each other. Each axis extends over the entire screen, the *X* (horizontal) from top to bottom and the *Y* (vertical) from left to right. The axes can be measured as the dimensions of the screen display. Their intersections create a continuous, unseen grid. The user is

aware of the grid because lines are created by moving the cursor from point to point within it.

Digital drawing uses **Bézier curves** with nonuniform arcs to draw curved lines and forms. The user selects two sets of **anchor points** on the screen and creates a pair of tangents, the Bézier "handles."[6] The direction of each curve is plotted by manipulating the handles (See Figure 4-12).

Horizontal and vertical lines in pixel-based (paint) programs are continuous, but curved and diagonal lines may be jagged or stepped because the size and shape of the pixels is determined by the software.

Lines drawn with vector-based (draw) software are not pixel-dependent. Draw programs have a closer and more continuous grid than paint programs. Draw programs are capable of generating smoothly continuous, near-flawless lines whether those lines are vertical, horizontal, diagonal, or curved.

Drawing falls into two principal categories: freehand drawing and technical drawing. **Freehand drawing** is interpretive and expressive. **Technical drawing** is formal and mathematically precise.

For most of history, drawing was done from direct observation. Tools for drawing, easily portable, were carried into the field by explorers and conquerors. Drawings were used routinely to record the exotic and the unthinkable. The nineteenth century exploration of Africa is recorded in drawings; Charles Darwin and James Audubon drew; the Civil War was drawn for newspaper publication by Winslow Homer even as Matthew Brady opened the field of news pho-

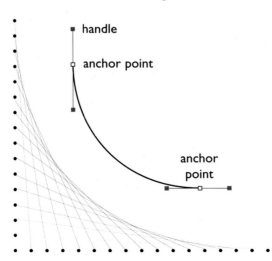

FIGURE 4-12.
Bézier curves are drawn from anchor point to anchor point guided by "handles."

handle

anchor point

anchor point

DESIGN FUNDAMENTALS FOR THE DIGITAL AGE

tography. Drawings are used today to record courtroom events where cameras are barred.

Direct observation is the heart of traditional drawing. Drawing can be rapid—it's possible to capture the essence of a an object or moment in a quick sketch, and the spontaneous quality of many drawings arises from the speed with which they were executed (See Figure 4-13). Studies and studio drawing are a more painstaking way to delineate directly observed subjects. Pictorial depth cues help to resolve the difficulties associated with interpreting solid objects.[7]

Many contemporary drawings disregard observation entirely, using drawing to express emotions or ideas in nonrepresentational ways (See Figure 4-14). Whether a drawing is a rapid sketch or a detailed study, representational or nonrepresentational, observed or felt, if it emerges from a hand implement used directly on a surface, it is a drawing done in a traditional way. The sensory impact of a traditional drawing is influenced by materials and techniques. Irregular surfaces like rough paper have actual depth. They create surface light and shadow that is unrelated to the drawing itself. Unplanned breaks in drawing occur as a tool skips on a rough surface; this too contributes an impression of depth and texture. Uneven pressure on a drawing tool transfers varying amounts of a medium to the drawing surface. Texture invites touch, increasing the extent of sensory appeal.

Changes and erasures on a traditional drawing leave visible traces. The surest drawing hand wavers at times. All of these accidental qualities of materials and technique combine to soften

A

B

FIGURE 4-13.
Spontaneous self-portraits capture the moment. (a) drawing, (b) digital drawing.

FIGURE 4-14.

A nonrepresentation-
al drawing of soft,
indistinct lines is
barely separated from
its background. It
seems to have texture
and to float in space.

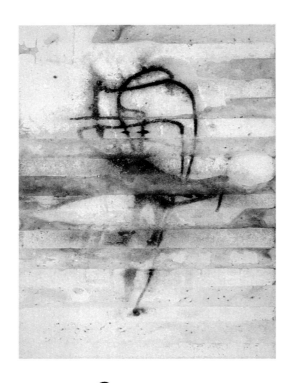

FIGURE 4-15.

The crisp, hard lines
of this digital draw-
ing loop freely to cre-
ate a simultaneous
impression of volume
and weightlessness.

and humanize even the most controlled of drawings. The warm visual qualities of traditional
freehand drawings are a reflection of the ways
they are made.

The computer is not (yet) a medium that can
be carried in a pocket. Computers are not
portable in the same way as pencils or pens. The
computer and its accessories are used most easily
when they are connected to each other in a single location.

The subject matter of most computer drawing is often indirectly observed. Many digital
drawings originate from scanned images, from
imagination, or from electronic or printed
sources. Digital drawing does not often involve
direct observation of a subject (See Figure 4-15).

Spontaneity in digital drawing is easily
achieved, but the warmth of human error is
reduced or absent. Lines drawn in light are infi-
nitely correctable. Once deleted, they leave no
trace. Texture is not possible in a screen image. A
surface can be dappled with fragmented light
and color, but a digital drawing cannot have on-
screen texture (although it can be printed onto
textured paper).

Digital drawing appears on a screen that is
remote from the hand that creates it. The
eye–hand coordination that is the essence of the
act of drawing must be learned in a new way.

Digital freehand drawing is too new to have a
history. Techniques develop and are superseded
almost at once by new capabilities. Digital freehand drawing is a still-emerging set of conventions.

Technical drawings are hand drawn by lines made against a guide—a straight edge, stencil, or template (See Figure 4-17). The guided lines of a technical drawing are meant to be flawless. The goal of a technical drawing is to communicate information, and its standard of excellence is a perfectly controlled line. The same attribute that diminishes the appeal of the digital medium for freehand drawing—the lack of human error—is a virtue in the production of technical drawings (See Figure 4-16).

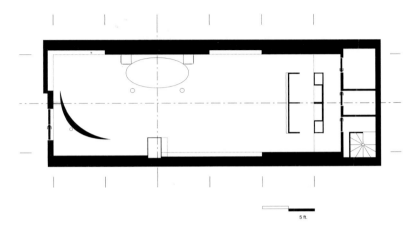

FIGURE 4-16. *The hard lines of digital technical drawings are near-flawless.*

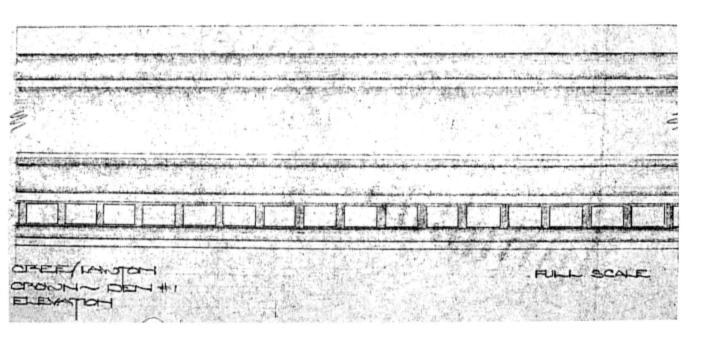

FIGURE 4-17.
Detail of dentil molding.

Form and Shape

A **form** is a single figure that has been reduced to its essential mass, contours, or area. A form is a visual summary. It provides general information about something without identifying it individually. A form can be distinguished from one that is unlike it—a human form is not mistaken for a kangaroo—but it cannot be identified as a specific individual. Forms are differentiated by their size, mass, contours, area, and proportions.

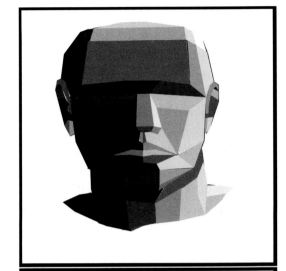

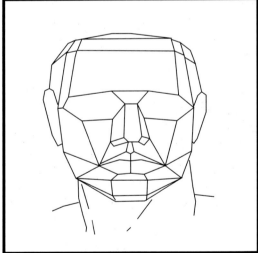

FIGURE 4-18. *A solid is a three-dimensional form. This head is a solid constructed of intersecting planes.*

Closed-path lines isolate **two-dimensional forms** from their background. A two-dimensional **mass** is an expanse of tone or color that covers the area of a form.

Three-dimensional forms are **solids.** A solid has a continuous surface and is physically separate in space (See Figures 4-18 and 4-19). A solid may have **voids,** or openings within it, but it maintains its wholeness and separation from other forms. A **three-dimensional mass** is a solid that gives an impression of weight, density, or bulk.

A **shape** has individual identity. Small variations in size, proportion, internal pattern, and surface give shapes their individuality. Forms are simplified. Shapes are detailed.

Forms and shapes are understood as things separated from a background, a perception called figure-ground separation. Form and shape are aspects of recognition. Searching for Elsie in a herd of cows and sheep, the form "cow" is recognized first as different from the form "sheep." Elsie has an individual shape. Her tail is curled, one horn is crooked, and she has a pattern of spots that make her distinguishable from the rest of the cows.

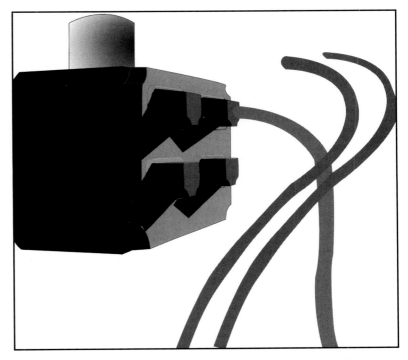

FIGURE 4-19. *Planes and value (but no lines) are used to illustrate a electrical socket.*

Abstraction

Abstraction is the reduction of something to its essential form. Abstraction reduces a figure to a simpler idea. The most distinctively proportioned or detailed entity can be simplified to the point where it is a form (See Figure 4-20).

The starting point of abstraction is the uniqueness of the individual shape. Its end point is the generality of form. Between these two poles figures can be represented at lesser and greater levels of abstraction: some closer to the sharp definition of specific shape, others closer to the generality of form.

FIGURE 4-20.
A shape is a figure with individual identity. A form can be distinguished from another form but not identified individually. Abstraction defines what is essential about a shape and reduces it to the simplicity of form.

Pure Form

The extreme of abstraction is pure form. A **pure form** is a figure reduced to its absolutely simplest manifestation. Detail and ornament are stripped away to display only the largest possible idea.

Pure form is the most powerful way to communicate structural ideas. It is the visual expression of Gestalt theory. A great deal of twentieth-century design reflects this concept as an aesthetic ideal. Pure form can be found in the uninterrupted planes of a building, the simplicity of a Calvin Klein suit, a dinner plate without ornamentation, the simplified letter forms of Helvetica type, a Raymond Lowy toaster (See Figure 4-21). Every design discipline has been influenced in some way by the hypothesis that pure form is the perfection of simplicity—or, perhaps, the simplicity of perfection.

FIGURE 4-21. *The rectilinear mass of the World Trade Center comes close to an ideal of pure form.*

Size

A **dimension** is a measurement in a single direction. The **size** of something is the physical reality of its complete dimensions.

Dimensions are described in terms of position in space. Two-dimensional forms are described as having width, a side-to-side (left-to-right, or horizontal) dimension, and height, a dimension measured vertically from top to bottom.

Conveying an object's dimensions using words alone is risky. In a two-dimensional form with one dimension much greater than the other (like an extended rectangle), the longer dimension may be called "length," and "width" used to described the shorter dimension, even if it is vertical. Describing the dimensions of three-dimen-

sional forms is even more problematical. Objects are described in terms of their vertical, horizontal, and depth dimensions, but information based on vertical, horizontal, and depth becomes unclear when a form or object is rotated in space (See Figure 4-22).

When the dimensions are critical pieces of information, only dimensioned diagrams will report that information reliably.

FIGURE 4-22.
Dimensioned drawings are the most reliable way to communicate the size of an object.

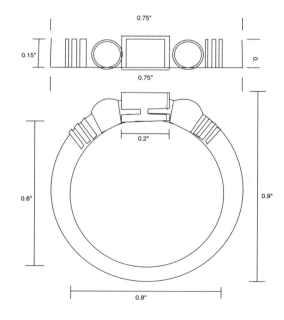

Scale

Scale is the size of one thing relative to another, different thing. It is a relationship of comparison that requires a point of reference.

Drawings in scale use actual dimensions for reference. A drawing scaled as "¼″ = 1′″ means that each ¼″ on the drawing represents 1′ of real space. Objects in the real world are not so conveniently labelled. Conclusions about the scale of actual objects and spaces require an objective reference. The usual reference for scale is the human figure. Most objects in the manmade environment are sized to be physically and emotionally comfortable for human use. They are in **human scale.**

Things that deviate from human scale provoke an emotional response. Objects in **miniature scale** are too small for human use. An object in miniature scale can be endearing and precious, like a dollhouse. Alternatively, small objects can make an observer feel awkward and uncomfortable. A tiny, delicate chair is unwelcoming. It is understood as too fragile to support ordinary weight.

Objects and spaces in **monumental scale** are larger than needed for the human figure. Monumental scale intimidates. It is meant to dominate and awe, to convey a sense of majesty, to reduce the observer to relative insignificance. It is the scale of Imperial Rome, of cathedrals, palaces, and courthouses (See Figure 4-23).

The human figure is only one possible point of reference for scale. The context in which something is seen can provide an alternative to human scale. A dollhouse with a doll in it is in scale for the doll; its rooms can be monumental relative to their tiny occupant.

Hieratic scale uses relative size to indicate status. In hieratic scale actual size relationships are disregarded. Important elements are larger and less important ones are smaller. Many children's drawings exhibit hieratic scale unconsciously, showing family members in sizes that reflect their importance to the child without regard for physical reality. The use of hieratic scale in design is commonplace, particularly in architecture, interior design, landscape, and stage design. Symbolically important spaces and objects are made larger than less important ones. The presi-

FIGURE 4-23. *Monumentally scaled structures and objects are meant to dominate the observer (look for the tiny figure to the left of the doorway).*

dent's office is larger than the vice president's even if the vice president needs more room. The throne is larger than the chair whether or not the monarch is smaller than the guest (See Figure 4-24).

FIGURE 4-24. *The Pharaoh is shown in hieratic scale—considerably larger than his wife, an indication of his greater (self) importance.*

Proportion is an internal relationship of the parts of a whole. Proportion is the relative size of the parts of a complete entity. Joe and Steve are the same height and weight, but Joe's legs are six inches longer than Steve's. Their bodies are the same size, but each body is differently proportioned. Two four-quart cooking pots are different in diameter and in height; their capacity is the same, their proportions different (See Figure 4-26).

The Greek mathematician Euclid proposed a theory of ideal proportions that can be illustrated as a line, *AC,* that has an off-centered point located at *B.* The relationship of *AB* to *BC* is identical to the relationship of *AB* to *AC*[8] a proportional relationship of approximately 1:616. This ratio of "ideal" proportion is the **Golden Section** or Golden Mean[9] (See Figure 4-25).

Inevitably, the theory of ideal proportions was considered in terms of the human body. Vitruvius, a Roman architect, considered the proportions of Greek temples and their relationship to the human body; he also considered the human body in a variety of mathematical formats: of center, circumference, and square; of symmetry, ratio, and proportion. Leonardo Da Vinci's drawing of a man contained by a square and a circle, made 15 centuries later, is an interpretation of the Vitruvian figure.[10]

The medieval mathematician Leonardo Fibonacci, searching for a proof of Euclid's theory, devised a sequence of numbers beginning with 1, 2. Each number in a **Fibonacci series** is added to the one before it in a progression: 1, 2,

3, 5, 8, 13, 21, 34, 55, and so on. Adjacent pairs of numbers have proportions very close to those of the Golden Section: 1:2, 2:3, 3:5, 5:8, 8:13, and so on.

Palladian proportions stem from the work of the sixteenth century architect Andrea Palladio, who asserted that each area of a structure should have proportions in common with the exterior. The Palladian ideal is not a new theory of ideal proportions so much as it is a hypothesis that the recurrence of proportions creates continuity in design.

The idea that mathematical absolutes of beauty, balance, and order exist in the natural world is one of the oldest and most cerebral of notions. It remains alive today. Swiss architect Le Corbusier (Charles Jeanneret, 1887–1965) introduced "Le Modulor" in 1948. Le Modulor attempted to define mathematically a "harmonic measure to the human scale, universally applicable to architecture and mechanics." Le Corbusier based the proportions of his human figure on a combination of center line and the proportions of the Golden Section (See Figure 4-27).

Ideas about proportion, like those of Euclid, Vitruvius, Fibonacci, Palladio, and Le Corbusier, are *guides* for proportioning forms and spaces. That they are guides rather than rules is illustrated by the frequency with which they are abandoned when instinct suggests a better proportion. Le Corbusier wrote treatises on Le Modulor twice, once in 1948 and again in 1957, but never failed to abandon it completely when his eye told him it was not right. He once

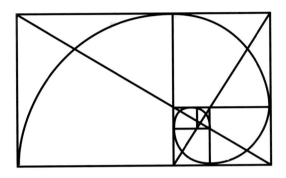

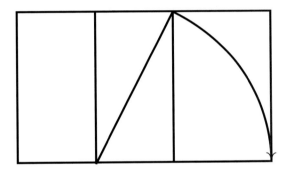

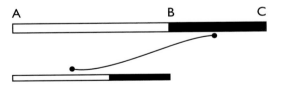

FIGURE 4-25.

The proportions of the Golden Section can be used to construct spirals that parallel those in nature.

banned the system from his studio altogether for a period because students and associates relied on it indiscriminately (Curtis, 163–64).

There are studies that have found a relationship between a variety of natural forms (fish, animals, plants) and theoretically ideal proportions. Both the Fibonacci series and the Golden Section can be used to construct spirals that parallel nature, like the spirals of the shell of the chambered nautilus. The concept of a natural harmony of proportions is a seductive one. Has an ideal ratio of length to width been discovered because it exists in nature, or is nature being described in such a way that it fits into theory of the ideal?

A preference for the rectangular form (over the square or round) seems to be natural to human beings. More tangible things (like paintings, books, magazines, paper, rooms, carpets, towels, boxes, trays, buildings, and furniture) are rectangular than any other shape. The dominance of the rectangle may lie in the simple fact that the width and height of the human visual field, 180 degrees horizontally and 130 degrees vertically, corresponds in form to the proportions of Euclid and Fibonacci. The field of vision is a rectangle.

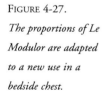

FIGURE 4-27.

*The proportions of Le
Modulor are adapted
to a new use in a
bedside chest.*

References

Cotton, Bob, and Richard Oliver. *The Cyberspace Lexicon.* London: Phaidon, 1994.

Curtis, William Jr. *Le Corbusier: Ideas and Forms.* Oxford: Phaidon Press Ltd., 1986.

Larsen, Jack Lenor, and Jeanne Weeks. *Fabrics for Interiors.* New York: Van Nostrand Reinhold, 1975.

Endnotes

1 John Bartlett, *Familiar Quotations* (Boston: Little, Brown and Company, 1980), p. 887. Speech upon receiving the Nobel Prize, 1976.

2 Ibid. p. 661. Thomas Edison.

3 See Gestalt Psychology, Chapter 3, page 52.

4 See **X, Y, and Z Axes,** Chapter 6, p. 102.

5 "Drawing" is a category of work with indefinite boundaries. Work rendered using brushes, or with masses of tone or color is generally considered to be painted, not drawn. The debate about what is a drawing and what is not can be fierce: One museum's planned show of "drawings" became such a battle over what was appropriate to include that it ended up with the noncontroversial title "Works on Paper."

6 Tangents are short lines that do not intersect.

7 See Chapter 6, page 100.

8 The longer segment is related proportionally to the shorter one in the same way that the longer is related to the sum of both.

9 A name given in the nineteenth century to Euclid's proportions.

10 Julius Panero and Martin Zelnick, *Human Dimensions and Interior Space* (New York: Whitney Library of Design, 1979), p. 17. Leonardo's contemporary, the mathematician Luca Paccoli, wrote a book, *Divina Porportione,* in which he associated mathematical proportions with "divine" aesthetic principles found in "architectural forms, in the human body, and even in the letters of the Latin alphabet."

Chapter 5

STRUCTURE AND SURFACE

STRUCTURE AND SURFACE / CONTRAST AND CONTINUITY / BORDERS AND MARGINS / NEGATIVE SPACE / AXIS / ALIGNMENT / ARTICULATION / EQUILIBRIUM / IMBALANCE / REPETITION / MOVEMENT / STATIC, DYNAMIC, AND KINETIC / PATTERN / TEXTURE

"One must not think that feeling is everything. Art is nothing without form."

Gustave Flaubert[1]

Structure and Surface

Composition means arrangement, or the placement of things in a organized relationship. Composition implies planning and control.[2] A car is designed (or composed, or arranged) of separate, planned elements—the curve of the fender, the shape of the door, the form of the hood ornament. The success of a composition depends on the combined effect of its **structure**—forms and their arrangement—and its **surface**—color, texture, and pattern.

Structure is the underlying arrangement of forms. Structure is the "body." Surface is the outermost layer of a thing—its face, or skin. Structure is *sensed,* but surface is *noticed.* An observer is aware of colors, textures, and of light reflecting from a surface.[3] Underlying structure is not so consciously observed (See Figure 5-1).

FIGURE 5-1. *Identical cube forms take on different personalities with a variety of surfaces.*

Contrast and Continuity

Contrast takes place when the independent elements that make up a composition also work to emphasize each other's differences. Contrasts of color, texture, or form; of ideas; or motion and stasis; even the nonvisual contrasts of sound and silence create excitement and tension. All compositions have contrast, even if it is only a contrast of dark and light. High contrast between design elements generates excitement. Low-contrast compositions are more serene (See Figure 5-2).

Line, plane, form, texture, and color are elements that are chosen, mixed, grouped, arranged, and discarded during the design process. **Continuity** is a planned association of ideas, forms, colors, or styles that serves to link individual compositions into a larger, extended whole. Continuity relies on the recurrence of some design component, but an element that lends continuity does not have to be repeated identically. A hotel design is an extended composition; public and private spaces are likely to share some stylistic theme. Product lines, fashion collections, advertising campaigns, and publications all exhibit planned continuity.

FIGURE 5-2. *A early Swiss door handle has a simple and elegant composition of contrasting forms.*

Borders and Margins

A composition has a visually logical beginning and end. Two-dimensional compositions are defined by borders or margins. **Borders** are lines that enclose a composition and separate it from surrounding space. A border can be a single line or a heavy frame. Everything within a border is part of the composition, everything outside the border is not a part of it (See Figure 5-3).

A **margin** is a border whose edges are not drawn. The edges of a margin are created by the vertical and horizontal alignment of compositional elements. Margins are implied lines that can be measured. The white space between printed text and the edge of a page is a margin.

An actor in a coffee commercial who turns to ask an unseen cameraman, "Can I drink my coffee now?" is stepping outside the frame of a performance. His action provokes interest by breaking the flow of information. Margins and borders frame visual ideas. Design components that break through borders attract attention by their unexpectedness (See Figure 5-4).

A three-dimensional composition is defined by its volume or the space it occupies. Solid objects stand separately in space (See Figure 5-5). The limits of interior volumes are defined by the planes that enclose them, like the sides of boxes, or the walls, ceilings, and floors of rooms.

FIGURE 5-3.
Borders are actual, defined edges. Margins are implied edges created by an alignment of text or images.

DESIGN FUNDAMENTALS FOR THE DIGITAL AGE

FIGURE 5-4. *Borders frame a composition. Something that pops through a border creates a visual surprise.*

A

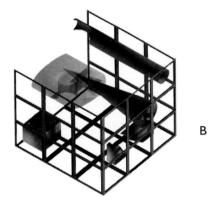

B

FIGURE 5-5.
Three-dimensional objects are separated in space. Here, a three-dimensional object (a) and a digital drawing of a similar figure (b).

Understanding something as a complete composition also depends on the setting and circumstances in which it is seen. A statue is understood as a complete entity until it is set on a dome, where it becomes part of the larger idea "building." Things do not change form in a new context, but they can change their roles.

Negative Space

Negative space is the area of a composition that is "empty." In two-dimensional composition, negative spaces are areas that are unfilled by forms or images. In three-dimensional forms, negative spaces are voids, empty spaces that occur as gaps or openings in solids forms (See Figure 5-6).

Negative space and filled space are equally important in composition. *Any arrangement of forms creates a simultaneous arrangement of negative spaces.* Negative space takes its contours from the unfilled areas within, between, and around figures. The areas within these contours demand awareness: they are inseparable from the arrangement of figures or forms.

Figure 5-6.

The unfilled area in a composition is its negative space, here as compelling visually as the images.

Axis

An **axis** is a sensed center line[4] (See Figure 5-7). It is the backbone of a form or composition. An axis is not necessarily straight. It can follow a curving path, even disappear and reappear as it moves behind drawn or real objects in space (See Figure 5-8).

The vertical axis is probably a response of the brain to the messages of binocular vision. Vertical axes seem natural. Planes have both vertical and horizontal axes that intersect at their centers. Volumes (solids and voids) have three intersecting axes—width, height, and depth. Their intersection at the center of a volume helps to give an idea its proportions and location in space.

Astonishingly, this "line that is not drawn between points that are not marked" plays a key role in composition. A single figure has an axis; a group of figures arranged as a composition also has an axis. Complex compositions have multiple axes—the "natural" center of the background plane or solid and the additional centers of the design composition.

A room is sensed first as having its center where the axes of its floor plane intersect. Doorways, fireplaces, and windows establish additional axes. Furnishings can be arranged in relation to one or more of the room axes or in ways that create new ones. The interrelationship of all the axes plays a great part in determining whether an interior design is sensed as a coherent whole or as a haphazard assembly of unconnected pieces of furniture.

An axis leads the eye. The points where axes intersect are focal points. A natural axis will disappear if design components are arranged in a way that establishes a stronger one. A location can be emphasized by axes that converge at the same point. Axes that lead in many directions scatter attention by giving chaotic "directions." The placement of axes is a principal way to control and direct focus in a composition.

FIGURE 5-7.
A single area of focus in a composition will shift the axis of the whole composition to that location.

FIGURE 5-8. *An axis can change direction and still be perceived as a center line. The axis of this garden is the walkway that carries the observer's eye through the garden.*

Alignment

Articulation

Alignment is also implied line. It is a sensed correlation between separate, unconnected forms. Alignment is a straight-line relationship between the edge or corner of one form and the edge or corner of another. Alignment also describes the relationship between the centers of two or more independent forms. Design components that are aligned on center have a common axis. Axis is a given, a factor that cannot be ignored.

Alignment is one of many possible ways to organize forms in space (See Figure 5-9).

Articulation is the joining or juncture of individual parts. Articulation is connectedness in the same sense that skeletal bones are connected. Forms can be articulated in a formal geometry or linked loosely to dance across space. Articulated forms are understood as *line*—they lead the eye (See Figure 5-10).

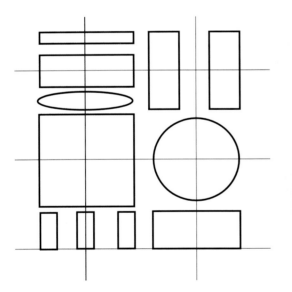

FIGURE 5-9. *Alignment is a relationship between unconnected figures. Figures can align at their edges or on center.*

FIGURE 5-10. *These dancing figures seem connected as one. Their arms and bodies create strong rhythmic movement as they dance through the painting.*

Equilibrium

Equilibrium in design[5] means that the elements of composition are in visual balance. Equilibrium carries with it the ideas of harmony, balance, stability, and order. A sense of equilibrium is brought about by the presence of elements of equal visual "weight"—forms or colors—on either side of a vertical axis.

Equilibrium is called a state of rest, but a composition can have equilibrium without being restful. Equilibrium is also **opposition**, the use of elements of equal strength to create a balance of thrust or visual force. Equilibrium is established in two ways: directly, through symmetry, and indirectly, through balance.

Symmetry is the oldest known formal arrangement of design elements. Symmetry is the arrangement of forms as rigid, reflecting, and measurable parts to the left and right of a vertical axis. Symmetry has a natural feel, reflecting binocular vision and the human form as well as many forms in nature (See Figure 5-11).

Radial symmetry occurs when the same element reflects repeatedly on either side of converging axes. The point where the axes meet creates the strongest possible focal point and establishes the composition's center (See Figure 5-12).

Balance occurs when unlike components of similar visual strength are arranged to create a sense of equilibrium. Symmetry is understood at once. Balance is sensed intuitively; it is not measurable. Balance demands more effort—the effort of eye movement across and around the composition and the effort of evaluating the visual information (See Figure 5-13).

FIGURE 5-11. *Symmetry is the oldest known formal arrangement, exemplified in this Romanesque door hardware.*

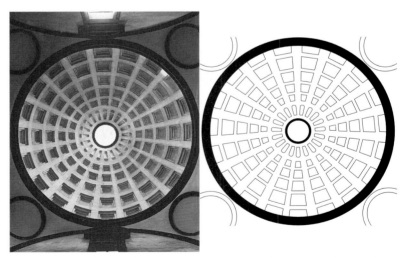

FIGURE 5-12. *Perfect radial symmetry in three dimensions: Michelangelo's dome in the Medici Chapel in Florence, Italy.*

Imbalance

FIGURE 5-13.
Balance is sensed as equal visual weight of different design elements. It cannot be measured.

If equilibrium carries with it the idea of harmony, **imbalance** conveys its opposite. Imbalance is unsettling. It creates a sense of unease and instability. Symmetry and balance have been considered virtues in design for so long that the power of imbalance is often overlooked. Imbalance in design is a way to create disorientation, to redirect focus, to disturb. Imbalance is a powerful tool.

FIGURE 5-14.
All utensils lead to the center to illustrate radial balance.

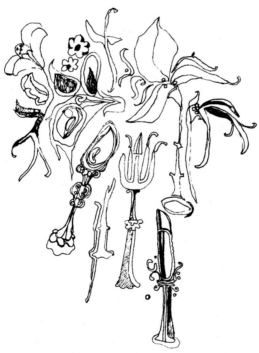

Radial balance is similar to radial symmetry. A composition with radial balance has unlike elements arranged so that all axes meet at a single point. Like radial symmetry, there is a strong, central focus at their point of convergence (See Figure 5-14).

Repetition

Repetition is the planned, uninterrupted, and regular recurrence of a design element with a maximum of sameness. Repetition is strongly related to structure—physical structure, as in the structure of buildings, and visual structure. Repetition gives an impression of stasis, of stillness. An evenly spaced row of identical columns or squares, or alternating squares and circles, is repetitive. Repetition suggests stability. What it does *not* suggest is action (See Figure 5-15).

FIGURE 5-15. *Repetition is the recurrence of a design element with a maximum of sameness. It lends a strong sense of structure.*

Visual **movement** is felt with the eyes. Forms can be arranged to create lines that move the eye across a composition and eye motion becomes an analog for real motion.

Rhythm is an *impression* of movement. Rhythm is established by design elements that move repetitively across, around, and through space, changing direction or emphasis at regular and repeated intervals. Rhythm does not demand exact sameness. It occurs in articulated forms and in forms and objects that are separated in space. Rhythmic elements can be interrupted. A sense of movement can be prompted by simple variations in the arrangement of forms. **Rotation** is a change in direction of a two- or three-dimensional mass without a change in form. A rotated form retains its contours but changes its position in space. It can be a mirror image, upside down, sideways, or at an angle (See Figure 5-10).

Axis and alignment help to determine whether compositions will be perceived as static or dynamic. **Static** compositions are literally and visually unmoving. They are passive and inert. Static compositions are strongly aligned and have a strong central axis. A static composition gives an impression of stability and order (See Figure 5-16).

Dynamic means "characterized by energy, action, or movement." Dynamic art and design is lively. It doesn't literally move, but its lines or forms suggest vigor and activity.

Dynamic compositions use lines and axes to provoke eye movement. Left-right is the first, instinctive eye movement. Up-down, and diagonal eye movements require more effort. Static images are perceived with a minimum of eye movement. A page of printed text is a static image, so is an igloo or a cube. Dynamic compositions use line to lead the eye in a dance back

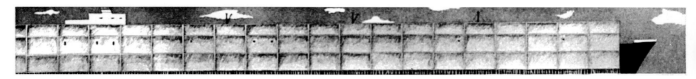

FIGURE 5-16.
Long, flat form without interruption holds a composition in place, unmoving and serene.

and forth, up and down, and across their surface. Short, strong lines cause rapid eye shifts that are analogous to agitated, staccato motion. Long, smooth lines convey a slower and more gentle movement. A drawing on paper, literally static, can have an enormously dynamic surface (See Figure 5-17).

Three-dimensional forms acquire added dynamism through the play of light and shadow. Shadows draw the eye in and out as well as across a form. Real shadows are line, mass, and motion—they form a new edge with each change in the angle of light. Even unrelieved flat walls can be invested with interest through a play of shadow. The Sydney (Australia) Opera House is a wholly dynamic composition: a concrete structure whose massive, curving diagonal forms, and the shadows they create make it seem to soar.

Kinetic art and design actually moves. Kinetic art can have two- or three-dimensional moving parts. Animation is flat moving images—kinesis in two dimensions. The computer medium is capable of representing the full range of stasis and motion: static, dynamic, and kinetic compositions—two- and three-dimensional.

FIGURE 5-17. *A powerful stone base is crowned by a child's figure challenging the sky. Inert materials are brought to dynamic life. Memorial Park, Hiroshima, Japan.*

Pattern

A **motif** is a single, specific design element; an individual image, form, or shape. A **pattern** is a reoccurrence of motifs over an entire surface (usually a plane). *All points on a patterned surface have equal emphasis.* The axis of a pattern is centered in the same way as the center of an unmarked plane. It is an "allover" composition[6] (Lauer and Pentak, 92). Pattern motifs can be connected or separated, identical or varying, arranged in staccato bursts or with rhythmic flow, but all patterns repeat in some way (See Figure 5-18).

The scale of a pattern may be too large for the reoccurrence of motif to be seen more than once. A **random pattern** distributes motifs in an apparently irregular way, giving an impression of arrangement arrived at by chance. Only hand-painted patterns can actually be created without repeat. If a random pattern is mechanically or electronically produced it will have a repeat, but it may have to be seen as a larger sample for the repeat to become visible. **Geometric patterns** have motifs spaced at regular horizontal and vertical intervals. The motifs of a geometric pattern repeat within the visual field.

Digital design is uniquely suited to originating pattern. Motifs can be multiplied with absolute sameness and infinite possible variations in size, scale of motif, rotation, and placement.

A

B

FIGURE 5-18. *All points on a pattern share the surface. An exercise in random pattern (a) becomes an independent composition. Geometric pattern, digitally drawn, repeats perfectly (b).*

Texture

Color and texture are attributes of surface. They are **finishes,** the last thing applied to a design and the first thing seen. Color is light, a completely visual experience and a principal field of design study. **Texture** is a tactile experience that extends its pleasures to the visual world (See Figure 5-19).

Texture is experienced visually as a mosaic of light and shadow. Light reaching a surface bounces off it, changing direction and scattering. **Glossy surfaces** reflect light directionally. A **specular surface** is an extreme of gloss. Light reflected by a specular surface is sharply directional and some of it reaches the eye as glare. Glossy and specular surfaces are visually tiring (See Figure 5-20). A **matte surface** diffuses light, spreading it evenly. Less light reaches the eye from a matte surface; matte surfaces are less tiring to the eyes.

A textured surface is rough, with small, irregular areas of high and low. Actual texture is experienced by touch. Rough surfaces scatter light in many directions, so texture reduces the total amount of light reaching the eye. A textured surface is a resting place.

The angle at which light reaches an object or surface determines the depth of shadows. Light coming from an acute angle, called "raking or grazing light," creates exaggerated shadows. Raking light accentuates texture by lengthening surface shadows. Even, diffused illumination minimizes texture by reducing shadows.

Texture is simulated on a flat surface by dappling it with tiny patches of light and dark that are too small to be separately distinguished. A

FIGURE 5-19. *Origami becomes a surface texture in a dramatic play of light and shadow.*

FIGURE 5-20. *Specular surfaces reflect light very directly. Digital drawing.*

simulated texture also reduces the total amount of light reaching the eye, but it does so in a different way. The patches form an optical mix that absorbs light irregularly rather than reducing it by changing its direction.

Digital design is not a particularly effective medium for conveying texture. In addition to its flatness the screen display is direct light and, although the monitor can simulate the light-and-dark patterning of textural shadow play, it neither absorbs nor scatters light.

Lauer, David A. and Stephen Pentak. *Design Basics.* 4th ed. Fort Worth: Harcourt Brace College Publishing Company, 1995.

Endnotes

[1] John Bartlett, *Familiar Quotations* (Boston: Little, Brown and Company, 1980), p. 583. Gustave Flaubert, Letter to Louise Colet, 1846.

[2] Configuration is another word to describe a planned relationship between forms.

[3] See Chapter 7, Color.

[4] Invisible or sensed lines are sometimes called **psychic lines.**

[5] Equilibrium has a different meaning in color study. See Chapter 7, page 132

[6] Allover pattern has crystallographic balance.

Chapter 6

WORKING IN SPACE

DEPTH PERCEPTION / REPRESENTATION, IMPRESSION, AND ILLUSION / X, Y, AND Z AXES / PERCEPTUAL CONSTANCY / ORIENTATION AND RELATIVE HEIGHT / RELATIVE SIZE, FAMILIAR SIZE / TEXTURE GRADIENTS / LINEAR PERSPECTIVE / OVERLAP / SHADING AND SHADOW / ATMOSPHERIC PERSPECTIVE / COLOR / MOVEMENT PARALLAX / SPECIAL EFFECTS / VIRTUAL REALITY / HOLOGRAMS

"The eye may see for the hand,
but not for the mind."[1]
Thoreau

Designers are faced with a paradox: A great deal of design "product" consists of pictures—two-dimensional illustrations of three-dimensional objects, like cars, soda bottles, articles of clothing, or buildings—but designers have to think in three dimensions and be able to communicate three-dimensional ideas. The difficulty they face is that most solutions have to be worked out as two-dimensional drawings.

Real objects are understood by their volume and their contours, size, position in space, and surface. Two dimensions tell us only an object's outline. Depth, real or simulated, is needed to inform us about an object's mass, location in space, and to help to indicate its size. An illustration that has apparent depth appears to occupy "real" space. Three dimensions suggest that an object can be touched, a more complicated sensory response than vision alone. Nearly all design disciplines look for ways to enrich drawings with some sense of depth, some sense of the tactile.

Width, height, and depth establish the position of things in space, but only width and height are seen directly. Depth, the third dimension, is perceived indirectly because the retina receives only two-dimensional information.

Depth perception depends first on binocular vision, or using two eyes, each of which sees from a slightly different position and sends a slightly different image to the brain. The difference between the two images is **binocular disparity.** It's possible to perceive depth using only one eye, but doing so is harder and it depends more heavily on other information. Look at a view through a window with both eyes, then study it with one eye at a time. The view is slightly different with each eye, and although the three-dimensional experience persists with one eye, the view is slightly flattened and more like a picture.

Depth perception relies next on visual information called **depth cues.** Some of these, called **pictorial depth cues,** can be used to suggest depth in ordinary pictures like drawings, paintings, and printed material—in static images on a flat picture plane. Other depth cues, including some of the most important ones, cannot be used on a static picture plane. They depend on motion, time, and certain eye movements (Goldstein, 204).

Representation, Impression, and Illusion

A **representation** is an attempt to capture some tangible reality in another medium. Something representational strives to copy its subject as closely as possible (See Figure 6-1). Portraits, photographs, and three-dimensional models are usually representational. An **impression** is slightly different. It attempts to depict some reality in a more general way, without specific detail or attempt to duplicate the subject (See Figure 6-2).

Representation and impression are not rigid categories. Most drawn images lie between the two, and whether a work is one or the other is immaterial in our response to it. A drawn object is recognized without being mistaken for the real thing. A drawing is understood first to be a drawing and only afterward as its subject.

An **illusion** is a purely visual experience that is mistaken for reality. Illusions occur because a visual stimulus misleads the brain.[2] An illusion is seen but does not coincide with physical measurement or other sensory verification. Illusions are not necessarily about three-dimensional images. Two-dimensional illusions, like a pair of lines that are equal in length but appear to be two different lengths, occur in many ways.

The illusion of depth is a bridge between a drawn image and reality. Although the very definition of illusion tells us that it cannot be experienced by other senses, three-dimensional illusions seem to invite touch, as if to prove their reality through a second sense. Artists have always attempted to depict depth on a flat plane. **Perspective drawing** is a mathematical set of conventions for depicting depth on a two-dimensional picture plane. Artists attempted to

FIGURE 6-1.
A representation attempts to reproduce some reality in another medium. Ingres probably improved on reality when he painted Napoléon, but Napoléon is unmistakably the subject.

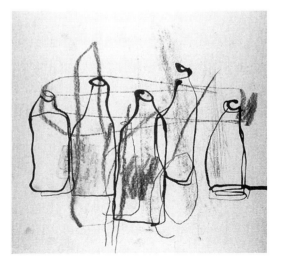

FIGURE 6-2.
An impression of bottles in a drawing.

depict perspective, with greater and lesser degrees of success, for centuries before a mathematical basis was determined for it in the Renaissance.

Static images like printed pages, drawings, prints, and paintings are limited to pictorial depth cues. Pictorial cues do not fool anyone into mistaking a plane for a three-dimensional form. It is always clear that the surface is flat.[3]

A screen image can include the depth cues of motion and time. The more visual information available—time, motion, and the full range of pictorial depth cues—the more convincingly the user can represent solid objects on-screen.

Software for solid-object drawing provides the monitor with a drawing field called world coordinate space, also known as object space, or Cartesian coordinate space (See Chapter 4, page 65). World coordinate space is a mathematically plotted grid for drawing three-dimensional objects. It is a reference space for the construction of three-dimensional models, the paths of light sources and animation.

Solid object drawing programs employ three axes called **X, Y, and Z axes.** The X and Y axes lie on the same plane at right angles to each other. In world coordinate space the X axis is horizontal and the Y axis is vertical. As in two-dimensional drawings, the X and Y axes can be measured as the dimensions of the screen.

The Z axis is a series of mathematically plotted points for depicting depth. Imaginary lines (connected points) along the Z axis appear to move back from the screen surface at a right angle to the plane of the X and Y axes. The user treats the Z axis as a spatial reality, but it is not. The Z axis is a very, very successful mathematical model, organized according to the principles of linear perspective, that constructs itself as an illusion (See Figure 6-3).

A monitor can be imagined as a hypothetical cube with one glass side, the screen. Each axis repeats itself continuously across the screen. The X axes extend horizontally across the screen from top to bottom and the Y axes extend vertically across the screen from left to right. The points where the X and Y axes intersect form a two-dimensional grid. At every point where an X and Y axis intersects, the Z axis also intersects, and a continuous, three-dimensional grid is formed within the cube.

Every point within the three-dimensional grid represents the intersection of an X, Y, and Z axis. Each point within the grid is a location "waiting" to be used in drawing. Drawing begins when the user selects a point on the screen and draws from that point to any other point, in any direction, within the grid.

Some drawing programs that use X, Y, and Z coordinates to illustrate solid objects rotate the coordinates, showing the Z axis in a vertical position. *A rotated position does not change the relative spatial relationships of the three axes.* The X and Y form a grid at right angles to each other in the same plane, and the Z axis intersects them on a plane at a right angle to the plane of the X and Y grid.

No one mistakes an on-screen drawing of an object for the real thing. The illusion is that the act of drawing is taking place in three-dimensional space and that the finished drawing exists in three-dimensional space. Solid-object drawing software is so convincing that it is actually called "three-dimensional drawing," and users perceive the screen display as having actual depth.

Some pictorial depth cues, like linear perspective, are built into programs. Other cues, like placement of objects above or below the horizon line, are part of the artist's input. Software with-

in reach of most design offices can produce convincingly three-dimensional effects on the monitor screen. Digital design has not erased the perceptual barrier between two and three dimensions, but it has closed the gap between the depiction of depth and the illusion of depth in drawing.

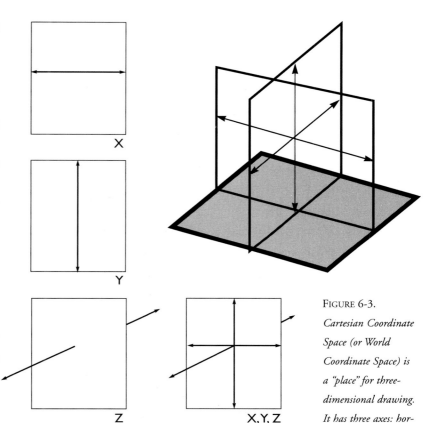

FIGURE 6-3.
Cartesian Coordinate Space (or World Coordinate Space) is a "place" for three-dimensional drawing. It has three axes: horizontal, vertical, and depth.

Perceptual constancy means that things are perceived as remaining the same even as our eyes receive changing images. An object appears to become smaller as it moves away. In spite of the direct evidence of our eyes we perceive accurately that the object has remained the same size and its distance from us has become greater (Goldstein, 232–34). Train tracks are seen to converge in the distance; they are nevertheless understood to be parallel. Perceptual constancy is a cognitive (knowing) experience that interprets visual experience. It makes possible judgments about size, placement, and motion in the real world (See Figure 6-4).

Our senses and experience combine to tell us where we stand (literally) in the natural world. There is an unconscious assumption that light comes from above and the ground is beneath our feet. Human posture plays a part: vision occurs near the "top" of the body, so near objects usually require that we look down and more distant objects cause us to look straight ahead, or higher.

The horizon is the place where the earth and sky seem to meet. The horizon is the "edge" of the earth and, like other edges, we sense it as a line. It is the boundary of vision, the farthest point that can be seen. Objects that are below the horizon line (whether they are in real space

FIGURE 6-4.

Perceptual constancy means that we understand things to be the same size even as our eyes receive changing images. Familiar objects are understood to be nearer or farther away, not larger or smaller, when the image changes in size. The distance of unfamiliar objects is harder to estimate.

or drawn) appear nearer when they are lower and farther away as they move higher and closer to the line (See Figure 6-5).

Objects above the horizon line are perceived in reverse. Things placed high above the horizon line appear nearer; things placed just above the line seem farther away.

FIGURE 6-5. *The horizon line is a reference point for the perception of far and near. Things are understood to be closer as they move away from (above or below) the line of the horizon. The sea appears closest to us at the bottom of the page and clouds seem closer at the top of the page.*

Familiar objects seem nearer or farther away because of what we already know about them. We know that an elephant is larger than a sheep; if the two are shown the same size, the elephant is understood to be farther away. Unfamiliar objects are more problematical. Additional cues are needed to establish their placement (See Figure 6-4).

Perceptual constancy determines that an object that is moving away is understood as remaining the same size, even though the image grows progressively smaller on the retina. The assumption that objects are smaller when they are farther away is a pictorial depth cue. The same form shown large and small is understood as being at two different distances away, not two sizes.

Texture Gradients

Texture gradients are depth cues that rely on familiar size, relative size, and assumptions about the location of the horizon line. Similar elements, like a beach of stones that are drawn closely together and gradually diminishing in size as they "move" from the bottom to the top of the page, are perceived as moving away. If the image is reversed, with the smaller stones at the bottom, the impression is that the stones are flying forward—the drawing has moved above the horizon (See Figure 6-6).

Linear Perspective

Linear perspective is a depth cue that relies on the perceptual fact that parallel lines in the same plane appear to converge as they move into the distance. This perception has been translated into a mathematically based, formal set of conventions called perspective drawing.

Perspective drawing begins with a horizontal line that defines the horizon, or farthest point that can be seen. A vanishing point is chosen on the horizon line. The artist selects a station point that is the location of the viewer. A station point

FIGURE 6-6.
Texture gradients demonstrate the viewer's assumption that the horizon line lies at the top of an image, or at eye level. Textural elements that gradually become smaller as they move up *on the page are perceived as ground receding into the distance. When the gradient is reversed, and textural elements diminish in size as they move* down *the page, the surface is perceived as above one's head.*

is usually (but not always) below the horizon line. The vanishing point is the eye level of the viewer at the station point.

Parallel lines that are meant to be shown as moving away will be drawn to converge at the vanishing point on the horizon line. Other parallel lines that are not moving into the distance are drawn as parallel.

The simplest perspective drawings have a horizon line, one station point, and one vanishing point. Real life has a multitude of choices: the height of the horizon, the viewer height and location, and the location of objects. Streets run in different directions away from us, and up and down hills. Perspective drawings can have two, three, or multiple vanishing points. Multiple vanishing points increase the complexity of a drawing and bring it closer to a representation of

FIGURE 6-7.
Linear perspective—parallel lines appear to converge in the distance. Perspective creates dynamic lines in a composition.

FIGURE 6-8.
Linear perspective.

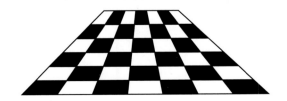

the real world, but they do not necessarily increase the impression of distance. The simplest drawing that suggests a road vanishing into the distance requires only one vanishing point and still gives a powerful impression of depth.

The mathematical basis of perspective drawing made it a natural candidate for transposition into design software. Vector-based perspective drawing programs, known as CAD (Computer-Aided Design) or CADD (Computer-Aided Design and Drafting) were the first design programs, and linear perspective functions are now a basic feature of software for solid-object drawing (See Figures 6-7 and 6-8).

Isometric projections are drawings that impart the idea of depth without attempting to

FIGURE 6-9.
In perspective drawings, lines that appear to be moving away are drawn to converge. In paraline drawings (plan oblique, elevation oblique, and isometric), all vertical lines are vertical and all horizontal lines are parallel. Lines parallel to X, Y, or Z axes can be measured. Paraline drawings do not attempt to depict reality.

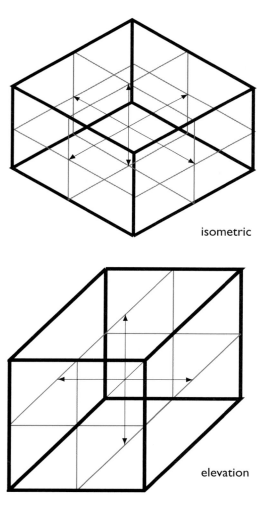

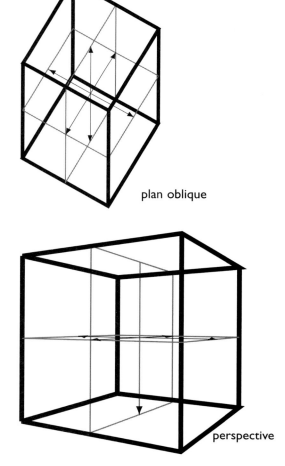

isometric

plan oblique

elevation

perspective

Overlap

show it as it is perceived in real life. Isometric drawing is characteristic of many non-Western traditions in the arts. In an isometric projection all parallel lines are drawn parallel, without convergence. Isometric projection is not a depth cue. Since all lines and planes in an isometric projection can be measured, they are frequently used for engineering and mechanical drawings (See Figure 6-9).[4]

Gestalt theory tells us that figures are perceived as simply as possible, so an "interrupted" figure, despite its incompleteness, is perceived as a whole. When forms are drawn as if they overlap, complete figures appear to be in front (closer) and partially covered ones seem to be behind the whole one.

Overlap is probably the simplest of the pictorial depth cues. It gives a sense of the relative placement of objects in space without any impression of object mass or volume. Overlapped images without other cues seem to be separated in space, but flat. Overlap is also known as **interposition** or **occlusion** (See Figure 6-10).

Hidden line removal and hidden surface removal are functions in design software that

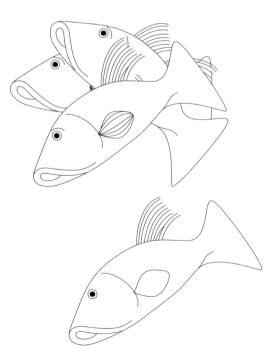

FIGURE 6-10.
Overlap suggests that one figure is in front of the other.

identify and suppress overlapped edges of lines or forms before they are displayed on the screen. The screen display of overlap and its function as a depth cue are understood visually as part of linear perspective.

The way that light reflects off the surface of a three-dimensional object is essential to the perception of its mass. Shading and shadow are pictorial depth cues determined by the direction from which light reaches an object.

Most of the time light comes from above. Unless there is contradictory information, forms are interpreted as if the light comes from above—and from an angle of approximately 45 degrees. The surface of an object is ordinarily understood to be lightest when it is close to the viewer and darker as it moves farther away. This generality holds true for figures that are constructed of flat planes; a darker plane appears to move away, a lighter one seems nearer.

A rounded three-dimensional form has "near" and "far" surfaces that are continuous. **Shading** is a gradient from light to dark that gives an impression of roundness or volume. The smoothness of the dark-to-light gradient is critical. If the steps from dark to light are separately distinguishable, the impression of roundness is lost and the image appears to be a series of overlapping flat planes.

Real **shadows** occur when objects stand between a light source and a surface. The area where the light has been blocked appears as shadow, or darker shape, on the surface. The angle of the light source relative to the object determines the shape and size of the shadow (See Figure 6-11).

A drawn or painted shadow suggests three dimensions by playing on some natural assumptions. A drawn object is perceived as within pictorial space,[5] but the light source is assumed to

A

B

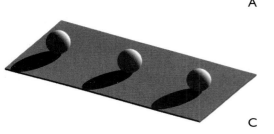

C

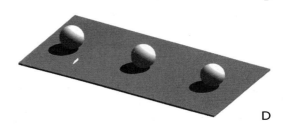

D

FIGURE 6-11.

The same image is understood to be concave (a) in one view and convex when it is reversed (b) because figures are interpreted as if light is coming from above.

Shadows and shading change their shape as the location of the light source changes (c and d).

be outside it. A shadow on the page is interpreted to mean that the drawn object is standing between the light and picture plane, and must therefore exist in front of the picture plane, in real space (See Figure 6-12).

Illumination from directions other than above is disorienting. Forms that are illuminated from other directions, whether they are in three-dimensional space or on a flat page, are interpreted in ambiguous or contradictory ways.

In addition to direct illumination reaching an object, smaller amounts of light reach it as reflection from other surfaces. A tennis ball cut in half, painted white, glued to a white wall at eye level, and illuminated evenly from all directions is invisible. Objects need the play of light and dark, seen as highlight, shadow, and shading, to establish their form and placement in space.

FIGURE 6-12.

Painted shadows give the impression the images are raised above the picture plane.

Atmospheric perspective is a depth cue that occurs when faraway objects appear less distinct than closer ones. The farther away an object, the more air and dust intrude between it and the observer. The air and dust blur distant contours, making them increasingly indistinct.

Objects also appear more blue as they move into the distance. The earth's atmosphere scatters more of the shorter (blue, indigo, and violet) wavelengths of the sun's light than the other wavelengths. This results in both the "bluing" of more distant objects and the blueness of the sky (Goldstein, 206–09).[6]

Colors have qualities that suggest depth. The depth impression of a color depends a great deal on its background and placement relative to other colors, but three general effects can be described.

Warm colors (reds, yellows, and oranges) appear to come forward relative to cool colors (blues, greens, and violets). Brilliant, clear colors will appear to come forward relative to more muted colors or grays, an effect that has a strong relationship to atmospheric perspective.

Value refers to the contrast of dark and light. In a two-dimensional situation, dark colors will seem to advance against a light background and light colors will seem to advance on a dark background. If a background is a middle value and

FIGURE 6-13. *If a middle-value background has both dark and light figures against it, the figure that has more contrast will appear to advance and the other will recede.*

has both dark and light colors on it, the color that contrasts more in value with the background will appear to advance and the one that is more similar in value to the background will seem to recede (See Figure 6-13).

Three-dimensional forms are understood differently. In a three-dimensional situation, orientation causes the viewer to assume that light is coming from above. The pattern of reflected light—the dark and light of shading and shadow—becomes the dominant cues to form. Lighter surfaces are perceived to be nearer, darker ones farther away (See Figure 6-14a).

A   B

FIGURE 6-14. *A three-dimensional trompe l'oeil illusion. The shallow stage of the Teatro Olimpico in Vicenza (1580, by Andrea Palladio) (a) was added by Scamozza in 1584–85. His success can be measured by contrasting it with the real depth of a stair corridor (b).*

Movement Parallax

Special Effects

Movement parallax (or **motion parallax**) is a critical depth cue that occurs when the viewer is in motion. Near objects appear to move by in a blur, but far away objects appear to move slowly. Distant signs can often be read from a moving train, but signs close to the track pass too quickly to be read. Objects are perceived to be near or far by a comparison of how fast they seem to move relative to the viewer's motion.

Design programs include a reasonable approximation of movement parallax. Screen images with movement parallax have one weakness. In real life the viewer moves, and eye movements are in response to viewer motion. On the monitor screen the images move, so the viewer's eye motions are slightly different.

A nineteenth-century school of painting called *trompe l'oeil* ("fool-the-eye") attempted to break down the wall between impression and illusion. Trompe l'oeil artists employed the standard pictorial depth cues, but in addition they limited the attempt at illusion to shallow images, like objects hung on a wall. Because trompe l'oeil paintings employ every pictorial depth cue and never attempt to convey great depth they are, at least briefly, very convincing as three-dimensional illusions (See Figure 6-14b).[7]

A stereoscope is an old viewing device that uses the depth cue of binocular vision to create a partial illusion of three dimensions. Normal focus at a near object is cone shaped, with the foveas converging to focus on the close object. Focus on the horizon occurs with the foveal vision nearly parallel, or the eyes looking out straight ahead. Eyes cannot focus in a diverging way (to left and right of parallel), but converging focus is natural eye movement. Stereoscopes isolate two slightly different images, one for each eye, as if the focus was parallel. The paired images in the viewing device are close to the eyes, so they are actually seen by converging focus, but because they are what the eye would ordinarily see with parallel focus the message received in the brain that the focus is parallel—and the view, distant.

Virtual Reality

The more recent *Magic Eye* books of images (by N.E. Thing Enterprises) create illusions of three dimensions on a flat page by extending the principles of the old-fashioned stereoscope. Magic Eye pictures use computer-generated, adjoining, vertical column pairs of printed images that shift slightly in focus. To see a three-dimensional illusion in a Magic Eye picture the viewer must force his or her eyes to look at the close image in a parallel way (as if to the horizon) and lock focus, restraining the natural impulse to converge. Unlike stereoscope illusions, Magic Eye images demand physical effort and the active participation of the viewer.

Trompe l'oeil effects, stereoscopic views, and Magic Eye illusions are partial illusions. They present near and far images with a partial flatness that is very like the effect of looking at a view with one eye. Objects seem to be placed at different distances in space, but solid objects are inconsistent—some seem solid, others flat. No one mistakes stereoscope or Magic Eye illusions for reality.

Virtual Reality (VR) is a computer-generated program that allows users to move, hear, speak, and touch objects in a simulated environment called Virtual Space (VS). Users wear special headgear, called a Head-Mounted Display (HMD) to "move" around the environment. VR images are not projected onto a screen. The images form directly on the user's retina, as if the retina itself is a screen.[8]

Each HMD has two screens that present a different image to each eye. The HMD uses the same principles as a stereoscope to counterfeit binocular vision, but since VR includes movement in the simulated world, a position tracker in the HMD generates this effect. The position tracker monitors the direction of the user's head and the direction the user is looking. The computer changes each screen image to match the user's "movements" at least ten times per second in order to maintain the illusion of natural movement.

Earphones in the HMD work with the position tracker to deliver sounds from "front," "rear," or the sides of the user. It also modifies the loudness and pitch to imitate distance and direction.

More than one user can participate in a VR program. Some position trackers can record motions and speech and send the information to other users. A microphone in the HMD allows the user to speak to other participants.[9]

Users can "touch" objects in the virtual space by wearing special gloves that have a position tracker. Objects in VS can be "touched" only in the sense of being encountered, surfaces cannot (yet) be felt. The environments in VS are so simplified that although the user is fooled into thinking that he or she is actually moving through space, there is no possibility of confusing that space with the real world. Further development of VR will make possible lifesaving training applications in medicine and time and cost-saving applications in engineering and design. The elaborate equipment still required by a VR program limits its present applications in design.

A **hologram**, (literally, *holo* = whole, *gram* = message) is a three-dimensional photograph that is taken with a lensless camera. Holograms are created by two separate beams from a single concentrated light called a laser. One part of the beam is directed at the object to be photographed, the other is reflected from a mirror or prism. The reflected beam creates an uninterrupted reference beam, while the beam directed at the object is interrupted at various points in space by the solid object. The holographic image emerges when the two beams, intersecting, create an interference pattern that delineates in light and in space the three-dimensional object that is being photographed.

Holography is capable of recording extremely fine detail. It is used extensively in medicine, in a technique called **interferometry,** for close comparison of two images of the same living thing. Holograms are also used with great effect as entertainment and for education. Walt Disney was among the first to make commercial use of holograms. At Disney World's and Disneyland's Haunted House's "ghosts" climb into a car with visitors. Visitors to New York's Museum of Natural History who peer into the opening of a simulated Central American mine shaft see a holographic miner chipping endlessly at rock walls (and with the addition of sound equipment, they hear him as well).

Holograms are illusions seen with the naked eye. They can be reconstructed in space in white light or in color. They can be static or moving images; they can be viewed from all sides. Holograms are, at this time, the only manmade

References

illusions that require no special optical equipment, gear, or physical effort.[10] They are true illusions. Holograms are not yet generally available but they are already emerging in the computer medium. It is only a matter of time before holograms will be seen routinely on the monitor display.

Depth perception may, in the end, be as uncomplicated as the Gestalt law of simplicity. Rudolf Arnheim proposes the most straightforward idea of all: *that a figure will appear three-dimensional when it is simpler to understand as a three-dimensional situation than as a two-dimensional one* (Arnheim, 248).

Arnheim, Rudolf. *Art and Visual Perception.* Berkeley and Los Angeles: University of California Press, 1954.

Goldstein, E. Bruce. *Sensation and Perception.* Belmont, California: Wadsworth Publishing Company, 1984.

Vince, John. *The Language of Computer Graphics.* London: Architecture Design & Technology Press. 1990.

Endnotes

1 Thoreau, Henry David. "My Life Has Been the Poem I Would Have Writ." *John Bartlett's Familiar Quotations,* 25th Edition. 1980. Boston: Little Brown and Company, p. 558.

2 **Hallucinations** are also perceptions that something is present when it is not, but there is no visual stimulus with a hallucination. Hallucinations are a product of the mind without a visual stimulus. A **mirage** is an illusion that is caused by atmospheric conditions. Mirages appear when light is reflected through layers of air of different temperatures, an actual stimulus.

3 A few drawings have been misunderstood—very briefly—to be truly three-dimensional. See Special Effects, page 114.

4 An early drawing technique called Alberti's window (also known as Durer's window) allowed artists to draw perspectives without the formality of horizon lines, vanishing points, and station points. A divided "window" with square or rectangular panes was placed between the artist and subject. The artist drew a grid with a similar number of squares and proportions, then drew into each "pane" what appeared in the corresponding pane of the window in front of the subject.

5 Chapter 4, See Pictorial Space, page 65.

6 Time of day also affects the color of objects. Fewer of the long wavelengths reach the earth's surface in late day, so objects appear bluer. A snowy landscape at the end of the day reflects these short wavelengths so strongly that it can almost vibrate with blue-violet reflection. Claude Monet's daylong series of time-sequenced impressions of the Rouen cathedral are a classic illustration of this time and color synchrony—the cathedral facade appears warm in color at midday, progressively bluer as the day ends.

7 Trompe l'ocil has been used decoratively in architectural interiors from earliest times (trompe l'oeil can be seen at Pompeii). It flourished in the Renaissance and reached an extreme in the Baroque period; many seventeenth century churches have solid domes that appear open to skies filled with clouds, flying angels, and saints.

8 Vince, John. *The Language of Computer Graphics.* London: Architecture Design and Technology Press. 1990, p. 148.

9 Funk and Wagnalls. *Encarta.* Microsoft® 1993–95.

10 Ibid.

Chapter 7

COLOR

"Who can doubt that colors exert
profound influences upon us, whether
we are aware of them or not?"

Johannes Itten[1]

Color is a visual experience that spans the disciplines of science and art. It is pure light, whether that light is seen directly or as light reflected from a surface. Color is experienced as a tangible reality because we disregard its cause and experience its effect. We believe what we see.

Color is useful. It modifies the perception of space and creates illusions of size, nearness, or distance. Color attracts the eye to establish areas of emphasis or focus in composition. Used symbolically, color communicates information. Color identifies or differentiates between objects of similar or identical form and size. It creates continuity in extended compositions. Color has physiological effects on the body. It can alter or induce mood. Color can be used to express emotions or convey feelings.

Most of all, color enriches the visual world. It embellishes the ordinary and gives beauty and drama to everyday objects. Color is a sensory banquet (See Figure C-1).

One way to understand color is to try to systematize it, to hypothesize and illustrate a color-relationship or color-order model. These systems fall into three categories: technical (scientific) systems, commercial sample systems, and intellectual or philosophical systems

Technical systems deal principally with light source colors. The information they provide is useful to industry but not especially useful to designers.

Commercial sample systems are devised for use by designers. Commercial systems don't offer all colors but attempt to provide enough for most needs. PANTONE®[2] Colors, for example, are standards of the printing industry. Pantone, Inc. produces colors in printer's inks with a corresponding range of products from color papers to markers and a palette for software, as well.

Intellectual and philosophical systems attempt to explain color effects. Historically these systems sought to construct a perfect color-order model and to find within that construct laws of harmony for color combinations.

Color theory is centuries old, but the line between the science of color (its association with physics and mathematics) and the art of color remained ill-defined until the recent past. Albert Munsell (1858–1918) devised a color tree based on perceived colors. The Munsell system, with an alpha-numeric "place" for every color and infinite room for expansion, is still in use. Artists of the Bauhaus, a design group founded by German architect Walter Gropius in 1919, moved color study further to a new focus on aesthetics. Bauhaus artist Johannes Itten (1888–1967)

The Color Vocabulary

retained some geometric figures in his organization of colors but also proposed a less formal system of color contrasts. Significantly, his 1961 book is titled *The Art of Color*. In *The Interaction of Color* (1963), painter Josef Albers (1888–1976) broke with the color-order tradition in favor of intuitive color exercises. Albers taught that the visual experience was paramount. Few color-theory systems are contradictory, and the best courses of study today include a variety of formal and intuitive exercises.

The **color vocabulary** translates the visual experience of color into words. It describes the qualities that are seen in colors and makes it possible to characterize differences between them. Every color sample has three qualities: **hue,** the name of the color; **value,** its relative lightness or darkness; and **saturation,** its dull or vivid quality.

Subtractive media like paints and dyes produce color by reflected light. Digital design uses direct light as a color medium. The skills required for mixing colors in any medium, subtractive or additive, are "how-to" skills that are specific for each medium.

The vocabulary that describes color is universal for all media and all design disciplines. Colors described as "mixed" are *visual* mixes, not recipes. The instrument used in solving color problems in design is the human eye. The intuitive understanding of color that many people possess is reinforced by every fact about perceived color. Perceived color has an innate visual logic.

Naming Colors

Color Intervals

Every individual both sees and thinks of colors slightly differently. No color name has exactly the same meaning for everyone. Even if everyone saw and thought of colors in the same way, the existence of monitors that display more than 17 million distinguishable variations in color is a reminder that a name for every color is a practical impossibility.

The color names *red, orange, yellow, green, blue,* and *violet* (or *purple*) are words for enormous families of related colors. A thing is called red when it is simply more red than it is anything else. We accept that something is red by unspoken agreement, common experience, and common language. No one calls a red apple blue.

Red, orange, yellow, green, blue, and *violet* are the only words needed to describe hue. A color "is" its most apparent or dominant hue. It can be more closely described by using the word *contains*. Color samples "contain" hues in varying proportions: "this red contains some orange; the other red contains some violet."

Intervals, or steps of change, can be set up between any two colors: those with hue difference, like red and blue; or value difference, like black and white; or difference in saturation, like brilliant blue and gray-blue; or between colors that contrast in all qualities. A pale pink and a dark gray-blue have hue, value, and saturation contrast, but a series of intervals can still be set up between them. An **even interval** is the **visual midpoint** between two samples; no closer to one parent than to the other. Any two colors and their middle interval are a **parent-descendant color series** (See Figure C-2).

Hue

The Artist's Spectrum

Hue is the name of a color. The word **color** is used in two ways: to describe a complete sample including all of its qualities of hue, value, and saturation; and as a synonym for hue. **Chroma** means hue. Words like *chromatic* (having hue), *achromatic* (having no hue), *polychromatic* (having many hues), and *monochromatic* (having one hue),[3] all describe conditions of hue.

A **saturated color** is a hue in its strongest possible manifestation, or **maximum chroma.** The reddest red imaginable, or the bluest blue, are saturated colors. Saturated colors are also called pure colors or full colors. Saturated hues can be diluted by making them lighter (tints), darker (shades), or duller (muted colors), but hues that have been diluted in any way are no longer saturated colors.

The **artist's spectrum** is a color-order system (See Figure 7-1). It illustrates the full range of visible hues in a circle. The basic artist's spectrum is made up of six saturated colors: red, orange, yellow, green, blue, and violet. The artist's spectrum is also called the **color circle**[4] (Hope, 201) (See Figure C-3).

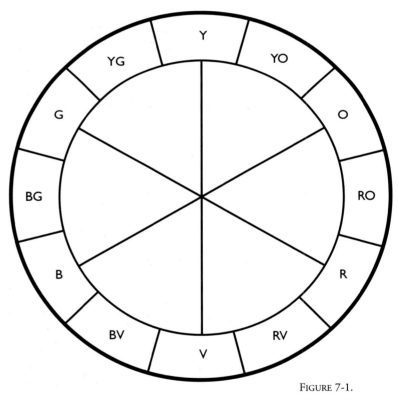

FIGURE 7-1.

The Artist's Spectrum.

The seven-hue spectrum of light (science) is linear, moving from short wavelengths of light (violet) to long ones (red) (See Figure C-4 A, B, C). The six-hue artist's spectrum is circular and continuous. There are many color-order systems: other circles; systems based on a tree; a square or on three-dimensional forms; systems with different names for colors; or numbers of colors. Color-order systems are different only in what they emphasize. *All systems recognize the same colors and sequence of colors.* No system is inherently more correct than another. The artist's spectrum is used here because it is a simple, familiar, and widely recognized system of color organization.

Red, yellow, and blue are the **primary colors** of the artist's spectrum. Red, yellow, and blue have a maximum of hue contrast. They cannot be broken down into component colors. All other hues derive from visual mixes of red, yellow, or blue (See Figure C-4 B).

Green, orange, and violet are the **secondary colors** of the artist's spectrum. Each is a mix of two primary colors, an even interval between a pair of primary parents. Green is the interval between blue and yellow, orange between red and yellow, and violet between blue and red. Secondary colors are less contrasting in hue from each other than primary colors. Each secondary color has one primary in common with each of the others. Orange and violet each contain red, orange and green each contain yellow, and green and violet each contain blue.

The artist's spectrum is also illustrated with 12 hues, but doing so introduces no new color names. The **intermediate colors,** red-orange, yel-low-orange, yellow-green, blue-green, blue-violet, and red-violet, are the midpoints between the primary and secondary colors.

The six- or 12-color spectrum is only a synopsis of all possible saturated hues. A saturated color is any color along the perimeter of the spectrum. If the full range of saturated colors is imagined as a full-circle rainbow with each color blending into the next, every point on that circle is a saturated color. Red-red-orange and blue-blue-green are saturated colors as certainly as pure red or orange or blue or green. The number of saturated colors is limited only by human color vision.

Tertiary Colors and True Grays

Complementary Colors

Tertiary colors contain all three primary (or two secondary) hues. They are chromatic near-neutrals—very muted hues or "browns." The colors in this group do not appear on the artist's spectrum. They are not saturated hues (See Figure C-5).

True grays are a mix of black and white. They are achromatic and have no hue component.

Complementary colors are hues opposite one another on the color circle. The two are called complements or a complementary pair. Every hue has a complement that is its opposite on the color circle. The basic complementary pairs of the artist's spectrum are red and green, yellow and violet, and blue and orange.

Each basic complementary pair is made of three primary colors: one as a primary, the other two mixed as a secondary. The basic pairs have complete hue contrast (neither half contains a hue in common with its opposite). In all other pairs each half contains a common hue. Blue-green and red-orange are complements and each contains yellow; blue-violet and yellow-orange are complements and each contains red.

The complementary relationship is about hue alone. Complementary colors retain that relationship whether they are pure hues, tints, shades, or muted colors. The eye reinforces any existing complementary relationship, no matter how muted or slight. A blue-green sample placed on red appears more green. The same blue-green placed on orange appears more blue. Muted colors with complementary contrast seem more chromatic and more different from each other when placed together. If a rose-gray is placed next to green-gray, each appears more chromatic: a much redder rose-gray, a much greener green-gray (See Figure C-6).

Analogous Colors

Warm and Cool

Analogous colors are hues adjacent on the spectrum. Analogous colors have been defined as a primary color, a secondary color, and any hues between the two, but this definition is limiting. Yellow-orange, orange, and red-orange is an analogous group that has no primary color. Another way to describe the analogous relationship is to say that analogous colors contain two primary colors but never the third, and a single hue is dominant in the group because it is present in every sample.

Analogous colors retain that relationship whether they are saturated hues, tints, shades, or muted colors (See Figure C-7).

Hues are characterized as warm or cool. Red, yellow, or orange predominates in **warm colors.** **Cool colors** contain blue, green, or violet. Blue is the polar extreme of cool; orange is the polar extreme of warm. The warmth or coolness of a hue is sometimes called its **color temperature.**[5] The spectrum is weighted toward the warm colors. Only blue is cool; red and yellow are both warm (See Figure C-8).

Warmth and coolness in hue are relative qualities. Green is cool next to red but can be described as warmer than blue. Even primary colors vary in warmth or coolness; a sample that is unmistakably red can be described as cooler (closer to violet) or warmer (closer to orange) (See Figure C-9).

Value

Value means relative light and dark in a sample. Value is about the light intensity of a color. A scale of value is a linear progression from light to dark. Value is most easily understood without the presence of hue. Black is the lowest possible value, white is the highest possible value, and middle gray (the middle interval between black and white) is a middle value.

The artist's spectrum was devised for subtractive colors, and value in a subtractive color is a measure of light *reflectance*. In the additive medium of digital design, values change with the amount of luminance, or light *emission*. Tints in subtractive colors are created by adding white, and in additive media by adding light. Differences in how tints and shades are "mixed" are immaterial. Value describes relative dark and light no matter what medium is used.

A value scale of even steps of dark to light is a succession of ever-doubling steps. Each step in a scale of even values is half as dark as the one before it and twice as dark as the one after it: a progression of 1, 2, 4, 8, 16, 32, 64, and so on (See Figure 7-2).

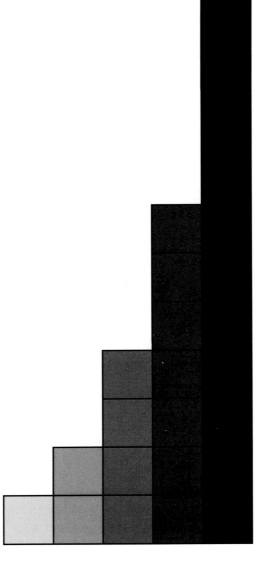

FIGURE 7-2.
Each interval of value is twice as dark as the one before and half as dark as the one after it; a series of ever-doubling steps in perception.

Tints and Shades

Saturated Colors and Value

When a pure color is changed in value, it is no longer a saturated color. A pure hue made lighter is a **tint.** A pure color made darker is a **shade.** A single hue illustrated in a full range of tints and shades is a **monochromatic value scale.**

Slightly tinted hues can be intensified color experiences. They contain a near-maximum of hue and have added light; as a result they are often mistaken for saturated color. Very light tints contain a minimum of hue. Sometimes hue can only be detected in a very light tint when the sample is compared to white.

Shades are reduced-color experiences. The reduction in light makes them both darker and reduced in hue. Slightly shaded hues are rarely mistaken for saturated colors. Many people find it difficult to associate yellows and colors containing yellow with their shades because the essential nature of yellow is so luminous, so opposite to dark. Yellow, like all other hues, can be illustrated in the full range of values, from near-white to near-black.

The **saturated colors** are at different levels of value. They range from yellow (the lightest) to violet (the darkest). Only red and green are roughly equal in value. It is difficult to discriminate value differences when the samples are different hues. For hues other than red and green to be equal in value, one must always be lightened or darkened—made into a tint or a shade. Only a tint of violet can be equal in value to a saturated yellow (See Figure C-10).

Value and Image

Value contrast makes objects distinguishable from their background. Black-and-white drawings, newspapers, and black-and-white photographs are well-defined images. Hue is not a factor in the perception of image. People with one of the many forms of color-deficit vision function well in the seeing world because "color-blind" really means "hue-blind."

The amount of value contrast between areas in a composition determines the strength of an image. Black and white, the extremes of value contrast, create the strongest images. When there is little value contrast between form and ground the form is difficult to see. Without value contrast there is no visible image at all.

Every image, chromatic or achromatic, has a pattern of values from dark to light. To duplicate an image in new colors (for example, to change a picture from red to blue) the new colors must correspond in their value and placement to those of the original composition. Scrambling the placement of values within a composition—changing a dark area to a light one or a middle value to dark—changes the image even if the outline of forms remains the same (See Figures 7-3 and C-11).

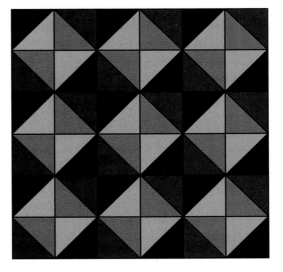

FIGURE 7-3.

The same composition has a radically different appearance when the value relationships are changed.

Saturation

Saturation is a comparative term for the contrast between a vivid color and a dull one. Saturation is relative hue intensity. A saturated color is a color at its maximum expression of hue.[6] A color reduced in saturation retains its hue identity but is duller, grayer, and muted (See Figure C-12).

A pure color can be reduced in saturation without a change in value. The interval between a pure orange and a gray of the same value is "gray-orange," a muted hue of the same value as its parents, but duller than the pure color and more chromatic than the gray (See Figure C-13).

A second way to reduce the saturation of a color is to blend it with its complement. Colors diluted by their complement are much more a part of our visual world than colors muted by the addition of gray. Nature is a chromatic experience, not a black-and-white one. When green fruits ripen to red or leaves turn from green to red in the fall they are illustrating colors mixing with their complements. "Nature shows such mixed colors very elegantly" (Itten, 50) (See Figure C-14).

When a *colorant* is diluted by even a small amount of its complement, it loses hue intensity and becomes duller (and usually darker). Adding the complement to a color in order to reduce its saturation and value is a classic technique in subtractive (paint) mixing.

Simultaneous Contrast

The eye seeks at all times to be in a physiological state of rest, or **equilibrium.** Equilibrium depends on the presence of the three light primaries in the field of vision (the red, green, and blue wavelengths). The subtractive primaries—red, yellow, and blue—reflect all of those wavelengths, so their presence in the field of vision also results in a state of equilibrium.

Equilibrium is destroyed when one half of a complementary pair is missing in the field of vision. **Simultaneous contrast** is the eye's involuntary response to stimulation by a single primary or secondary color. In the absence of its complement, the eye generates the missing color simultaneously and spontaneously. The missing color appears as a "wash" of color on an adjacent color-neutral area (See Figure C-15).

Simultaneous contrast is a continuous phenomenon. If a red design is placed on a neutral ground, the ground takes on—and maintains—a greenish cast. A gray paper square laid on an orange background takes on—and keeps—a blue cast. The same gray square laid on green appears as a pinkish gray.

An unwanted effect of simultaneous contrast can be countered by adding a fraction of the stimulating color to the affected neutral. A pattern of red on white gives the white a greenish cast. Adding a small amount of red to the white neutralizes the green that the eye adds—and keeps—the white looking "white."

Simultaneous contrast must be considered in the selection of every neutral (including, and especially, whites) that will be placed near a single hue or close family of hues.[7]

Vibration

Afterimage is a variant of simultaneous contrast. When the eye is stimulated by a single color that is then removed from the field of vision, the missing complement is seen (briefly) as a "ghost" image on a nearby achromatic surface.

The three primaries do not have to be equal areas of color for the eye to be at rest. It is only necessary that all three be present in some way in the visual field. There are endless color combinations and mixes that the eye accepts as equilibrium: three primaries, two secondaries, complementary colors, complementary colors mixed as muted hues, and others.[8]

The state of rest is reached most fully when the three primaries are mixed together as muted hues or tertiary colors. Reducing the chroma of a pure color makes it less stimulating. Muted colors may be used so often because they are actually *physically* restful.

It is technically true that the eye is at rest when all primaries are present, but a composition of highly saturated or brilliant colors may not achieve that result even if all primaries are present. Brilliant hues used together deliver separate, strong stimuli. The eye reacts to each as if it were an individual stimulus. The involuntary effort of the eye to respond to contradictory stimuli, to maintain equilibrium, causes optical vibration that ends as fatigue, headache, blurred vision, or dizziness.

Vibration also occurs when complementary colors of the same value are presented together. Value contrast separates figures from their ground. When two colors are identical in value, the eye has difficulty in finding an "edge" between them. Vision is experienced as a struggle and color as an assault (See Figure C-16).

The strongest color stimuli are those of direct light. The greatest risk of vibration and fatigue occurs in working with additive colors. Complementary colors of equal value displayed on a monitor screen can be literally painful to the eyes.

Ground Subtraction

Simultaneous contrast effects change in neutrals when only one hue is actually present. Complementary contrast reinforces any complementary relationship that already exists between colors, no matter how slight. In each case the appearance of a color (or neutral) is changed in *hue* by its placement relative to other colors in a composition.

Ground subtraction intensifies the differences between any qualities that a ground and carried colors have in common—hue, value, or saturation.

A ground is the background against which colors are placed. Ground subtraction depends on placement. When a color is laid on a ground, qualities of hue, value, or saturation that the two have in common are reduced and differences between them are emphasized (See Figure 7-4).

Ground subtraction is illustrated by selecting a middle interval between two parent colors and placing a piece of the middle mix on each parent color. Blue-green placed on blue appears more green: The blue common to both is reduced and the green remaining is emphasized. Blue-green placed on green appears more blue: the common green is reduced and the blue intensified (See Figure C-17).

FIGURE 7-4.

The same gray seen on dark and light grounds looks very different. The light ground pulls away lightness from the gray and leaves it looking dark. A dark ground pulls away darkness from the gray and lightness is left.

Optical Mixes

Color Compositions

Optical mixes occur when dots or patches of color too small to be separately perceived blend to form a completely new color. Scale and viewing distance are critical to optical mixes—the size of color dots must be close to (or below) the viewer's threshold. Optical mixing was brought to its gloriously logical extreme by the Impressionist painters of the nineteenth century, who laid closely spaced dabs of pure color directly on the canvas rather than mixing color on the palette. Paintings produced in this way often have a depth and liveliness of surface not possible with flat color (See Figure C-18).

The relevance of optical mixing to digital design is immediate and direct. Printers use tiny dots of color as optical mixes to achieve an extended color range from only four inks: process yellow, process blue (cyan), and process red (magenta), and black (see page 136).

A **color composition** is a group of colors meant to be sensed as a whole. **Color harmony** is the pleasing impression given by a color composition. **Visual impact** is the graphic power of a color composition. Both color harmony and visual impact are considerations in all color design. Harmony probably has greater application in long-term color uses like environments. Visual impact is the attention-getting color mode. It has an immediacy that gives it greater relevance to short-term uses of colors like fashion, signage, and package design.

Color Harmony

Balance and order were central to traditional theories of **color harmony,** which focused principally on the relationship between hues and, particularly, on the relationship between complements. Complementary pairs complete the need of the eye for equilibrium, but common sense tells us that any hues used together can be harmonious. This doesn't mean that any hues used together *are* harmonious—it means that there are no inherently bad combinations of hue, and that hue relationships alone are incomplete ideas about color harmony.

A great deal of what we find pleasing is controlled by involuntary responses. The characteristic of human intelligence to categorize information means that intervals, particularly *even* intervals, are visually and intellectually comfortable—easy to see, easy to understand. Groups of colors that are in even intervals of hue, values, or saturation, or any combination of these qualities, are inherently pleasing.

Brilliant combinations are exciting (they stimulate the eye) and muted ones are restful (equilibrium is easy to live with), but neither is more pleasing than the other. Most color compositions are pleasing when the level of saturation is relatively constant. Whether that saturation level is high or low is an issue of personal choice and intended use.

A composition with a reasonably even level of saturation is disrupted by an atypical element. A highly saturated color placed in a muted composition draws attention—the pure color jumps out. A single muted element inserted into a composition of pure colors is a blot on the clean, bright colors around it. An anomalous color stands alone as an area of emphasis, separated from the collective effect of the colors surrounding it.

FIGURE C-1. *Color embodies the richness of human vision. It communicates life.*

FIGURE C-2. *Two colors with a third color that is the visual midpoint between them. Series of colors in even intervals are easy to see, easy to understand, and play a large role in color harmony.*

FIGURE C-3. *The Artist's Spectrum.*

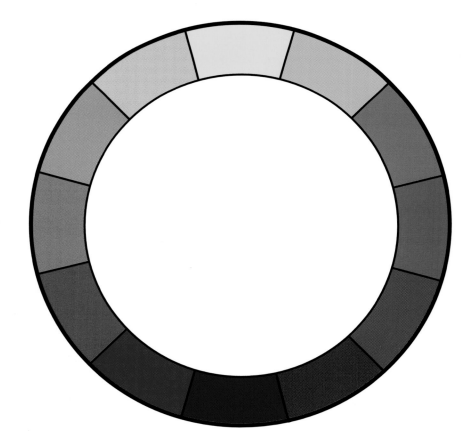

FIGURE C-4. *(a) The additive colors of light. Red, green, and blue are the primary colors of light. They mix to form the secondary colors: cyan, magenta, and yellow. All three primary colors of light mix to form white (or colorless) light.*

(b) The subtractive colors mix in a way that reflects most pigment mixing and echoes the artist's spectrum. Red, yellow, and blue are the subtractive primaries. They mix to form the secondaries: orange, green, and violet. All together they produce a dull achromatic tone, a near-black.

(c) Process primaries are a medium used in the printing industries and in computer color printers. They mix in a way that is different from most subtractive colors. Cyan, magenta, and yellow are the process primaries (also called process blue, process yellow, and process red). They are overlaid in different proportions to form all possible colors, but when all three are mixed they produce a medium-gray tone. Black is added in printing to give depth to images.

The process primaries do not mix to reflect a common wavelength like other subtractive mixtures. Instead, they absorb and reflect the light primaries. Magenta ink absorbs green light. Yellow absorbs blue, and cyan absorbs red. When magenta and yellow are mixed, blue and green are absorbed and the result is red. When yellow and cyan are mixed, blue and red are absorbed and green results. Magenta and cyan mixed absorb green and red, so blue results. All mixed together absorb all wavelengths and produce near-black.

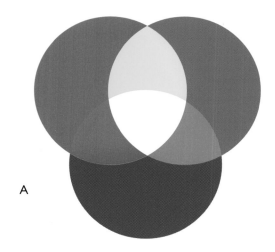

A

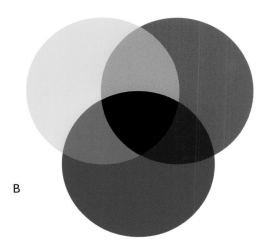

B

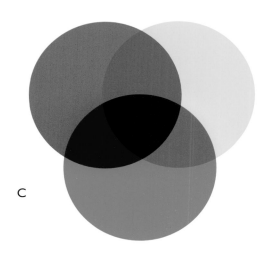

C

FIGURE C-5. *Master colorist Esteban Vicente uses tertiary colors as a background to emphasize the brilliance of clear blues and greens. Collage.*

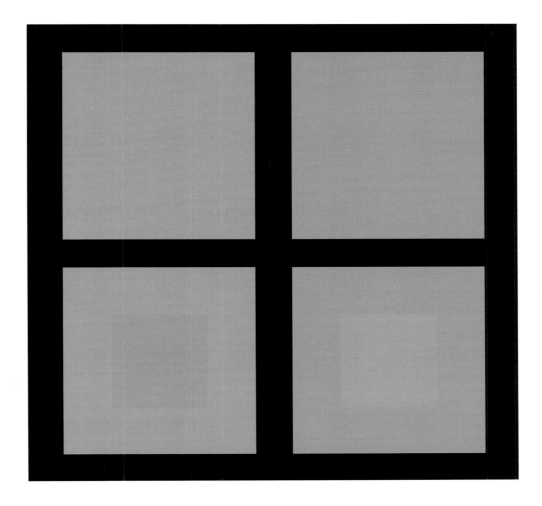

FIGURE C-6. *When colors that have even the slightest complementary relationship are placed next to each other, that complementary contrast emphasizes the hue that is present in each.*

FIGURE C-7. *Analogy is a hue relationship*
whether colors are pure hues, muted hues,
tints, or shades.

FIGURE C-8. *Warm and cool palettes in textile art: contemporary quilts (a) Summer Breeze in a cool palette and (b) Taking Flight in warm colors.*

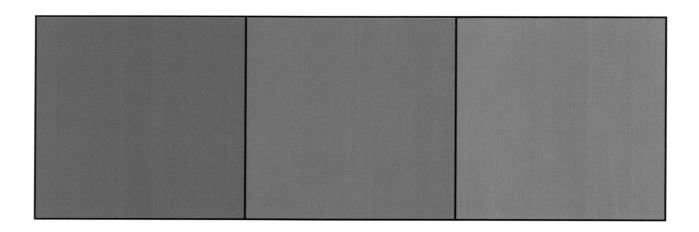

FIGURE C-9. *Almost any color can be viewed as warmer or cooler by comparison to another. Here, the red in the middle is warmer than the fractionally bluer one, and cooler than a fractionally more orange one.*

FIGURE C-10. *The pure hues are at different levels of value. The six hues of the artist's spectrum are arranged here to read horizontally as similar levels of value. Note for example, how the placement of pure yellow corresponds to a tint of violet.*

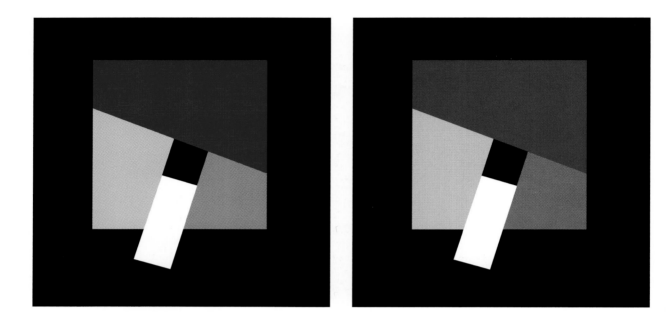

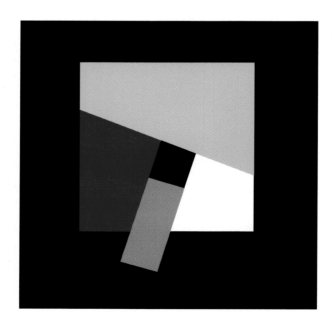

FIGURE C-11. *An image will appear the same in any hues as long as the value relationships are identical. Changing the value relationships creates a different image even when the same hues are used.*

FIGURE C-12. *Brilliant reds and oranges contrast sharply with muted ones in this early twentieth-century textile design stencil. Notice how the brilliant hues appear to come forward and the muted hues recede.*

FIGURE C-13. *Colors can be diluted (here, with an achromatic gray) so that they are reduced in saturation (chroma) without a change in value.*

FIGURE C-14. *Mixed complementary colors are muted hues. The visual midpoint of any pair of complements is a tertiary color, or chromatic neutral.*

FIGURE C-15. *Simultaneous contrast.*

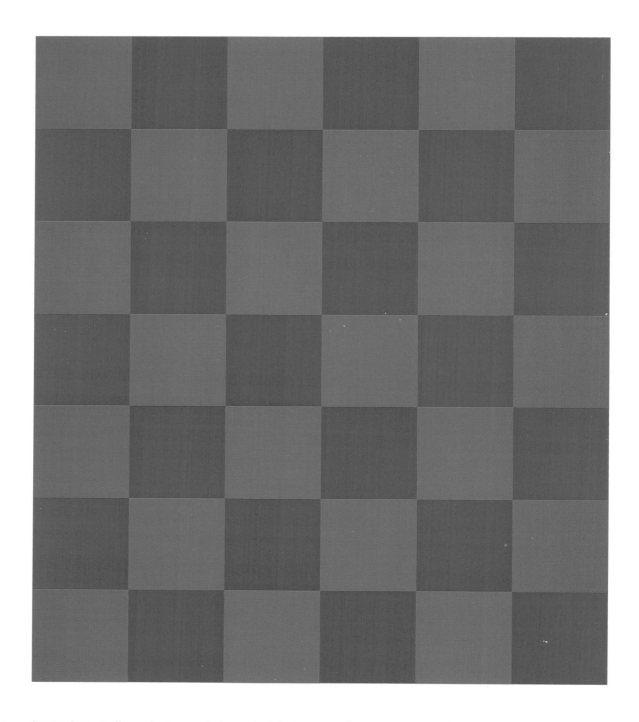

FIGURE C-16. *Brilliant colors (saturated colors or tints) that have a complementary or near-complementary relationship and are close in value will vibrate when placed next to each other.*

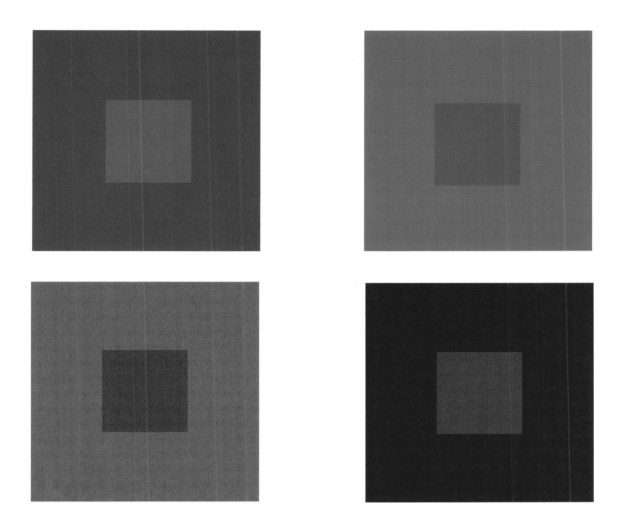

FIGURE C-17. *A ground subtracts its qualities from colors it carries. Whatever is common to the two colors is reduced and differences between them are emphasized.*

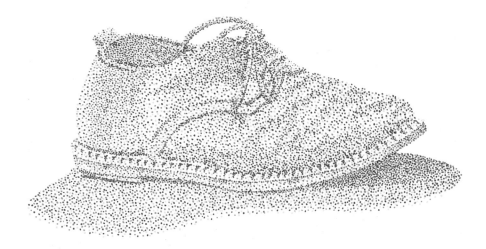

FIGURE C-18. *Optical mixes are new colors made from tiny bits of other colors laid close to each other. The viewer's eye, not the artist, does the work of mixing.*

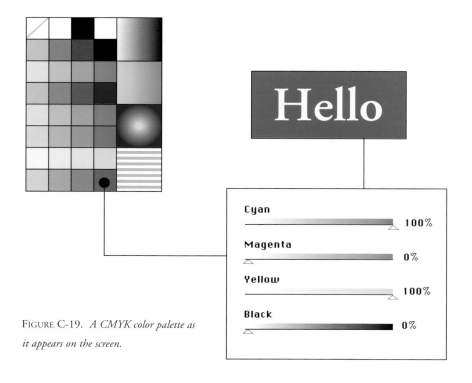

FIGURE C-19. *A CMYK color palette as it appears on the screen.*

Visual Impact

High-value contrast alone has tremendous visual impact. The eye is drawn to light and to strong pattern.

Color inserted into a black-and-white composition increases its force. Color images are retained in memory longer than achromatic ones; it has been said that a color image remains in human memory four times as long as the same image in black and white.

Colors that contrast strongly with the natural environment have shock value. **High-impact colors** are both hue intense and light reflecting. Red-violet and saturated yellow-green are examples of high-impact colors. Day-Glo colors literally emit light; they contain a substance that converts light that is beyond the visible spectrum into visible light. High-impact colors are likely to create vibration. They are good choices for attracting short-term attention, but poor choices for legibility.

Designing in Color

The end product of the design process is most often something tangible, like a book, car, a textile, or a building. The materials that give color to objects are subtractive media. Designing in color for tangible objects (including the printed page) often means creating a color composition in one medium for production in another. Selecting a medium for design rendering means selecting a set of capabilities, visual qualities, and limitations. No matter how competent the colorist there is always some disparity between the colors of a design rendering and the colors of the end product.

Dyes, Pigments, and Process Colors

A subtractive medium is a liquid, paste, wax, or other base that contains colorants. The selection of subtractive media is endless—poster paints, water colors, oil and acrylic paints, markers, crayons, colored pencils, dyes, and inks—and each has its own range of colors and visual qualities.

Dyes are colorants in solution. They are fully dissolved in water, alcohol, or other solvent. They penetrate the underlying material and bond with it on the molecular level. Many dyes are translucent and allow that material to reflect light back through them, so when used on a white ground they are very light reflective, or brilliant. **Pigments** are suspensions—finely ground particles of colorant suspended in a base. Pigments are opaque and generally more muted in effect than dyes.

Two or more subtractive colorants mixed together produce a new color in a simple way. Most colorants reflect two or more wavelengths. One wavelength is reflected most strongly, others that are present may not be visible to the naked eye.

A red colorant may absorb all wavelengths of light except the red and some of the orange; the red and some orange that is not evident are reflected. A yellow colorant may absorb all wavelengths except yellow and some orange; it reflects yellow and a small amount of orange. Again, that orange may not be visible to the naked eye.

When the red and yellow are mixed, each continues to absorb the colors it absorbed when used alone. The only color that can be reflected is the orange that both reflect in common. If

two colorants do not reflect a wavelength in common they will yield a muddy neutral when mixed, no matter how brilliant they appear when used alone (See Figure C-4 B).

Different hues within a medium vary in tinting strength. **Tinting strength** is the relative amount of the colorant needed to produce a difference when mixed into another color. In most media a teaspoon of red in a cup of yellow will make orange, but a teaspoon of yellow in a cup of red effects no change. The quantity of a medium has little importance in subtractive color mixing—only tinting strength brings about change.

Process colors (CMYK), are a subtractive medium used in printing. Process colors are available as color papers, drawing ink, marker, films, printing ink, and in other forms.

Color printing is done with the **process primaries**[9] cyan (C, a blue-green), magenta (M, a red-violet), and yellow (Y), plus black (K). Process colors mixed together do not reflect a common wavelength like other subtractive mixtures. Instead, they absorb and reflect the light primaries. Magenta ink absorbs green light. Yellow absorbs blue. Cyan absorbs red. When magenta and yellow are mixed, blue and green are absorbed and the result is red. When yellow and cyan are mixed, blue and red are absorbed and green results. Magenta and cyan mixed absorb green and red, so blue results (See Figure C-4 C). They are overlaid in different proportions to form all possible colors, but when all three are mixed they produce a medium-gray tone, so black is needed to give sharpness and

Digital Design:
The Additive Medium

depth to the color image. In terms of subtractive mixing, process primaries are close to the perfect medium. Two or three process primaries can be mixed in different proportions to yield nearly all possible hues and levels of saturation; the added black produces shades and additional muted colors.

Printers produce smooth, continuous fields and gradients of color through the optical mixing of tiny dots of process colors. The digital image (from the screen or from an image stored in memory) is separated by the printer into three bitmaps, one each for cyan, magenta, and yellow. Each single color bitmap duplicates the number and pattern of pixels of that color in the digital image. The bitmaps are printed out as dots and overlaid in different densities and positioned at different angles, which gives a reasonably wide range of colors. Black, a fourth bitmap, is added last to increase value contrast. The pixel dots of color mix optically to produce images of great color range, density, and depth.

The digital medium is unique. It produces images in the direct light of additive color to render products that will be produced in subtractive color. Design produced on the computer for distribution as screen images is unique in the opposite way—design medium and product medium are identical.

Programs display a basic assortment of colors in a box of squares, or **color palette** (See Figure C-19). The box ordinarily contains primary and secondary colors, some grays, and black and white. Palettes made up of colors that correspond to those of commercial color systems for printing inks like Pantone™ are also available, so designers working in the digital medium can use a palette that approximates that of a printed page.

Digital design resolves the problem of mixing the colors of the light display in three different ways: the CMYK mode, the RGB mode, and the HSV mode. Each kind of display has limits to its range of available colors called a **gamut.** Human color vision has a greater range than can be displayed by any of the color gamuts.

The **CMYK mode** (See Figure C-19) of color display is programmed to imitate subtractive mixing. Specifically, the CMYK mode imitates the results of mixing process colors. Each color in the CMYK mode represents a color available as printing ink and, as a result, it is a display mode that facilitates working on-screen for production in print.

The CMYK mode has a bar display that allows the user to select cyan, magenta, yellow, or black as a percentage of the screen display.

When one or two colors (CMY) are mixed without black, clear colors and tints result. The three colors, CMY, mixed in equal percentages without black make a middle gray. Muted colors are achieved by using the gray-CMY mix and manipulating one or two colors until the desired muted hue results.

A reduced percentage of black (K) used alone will also make gray, but a gray made with black alone cannot be mixed to produce muted colors. The black (K) bar is used for darkening. A mixture of one or two CMY colors plus black (K) yields shades. Muted colors must contain the CMY-gray mixture.

Varying the percentages of the three colors allows the designer to display a full range of colors including nearly all hues, values, and saturations. The CMYK mode requires little new thinking about color mixing for users who are accustomed to working with process colors.

The **RGB mode** of screen color display parallels the behavior of light. Each of the primary colors of light—red, green, and blue (RGB)—is displayed as a separate bar. The user selects each color for mixing in a range from no display (0 percent) to full display (100 percent). When 100 percent each of the three colors is mixed, the result is white. When none (0 percent) of each color is mixed, the display is black.

If 50 percent each of red, green, and blue is displayed, the result is a middle gray. Varying the relative percentages of red, green, and blue in RGB mixtures allows the designer to produce a full range of colors including nearly all hues, values, and saturations. The RGB mode is most

directly associated with reality of a light medium. It requires a new way of thinking about color mixing because the familiar techniques and results of subtractive mixing do not correspond to it.

The **HSV mode** operates in a different way. HSV stands for Hue, Saturation, Value.[10] The HSV mode displays a circular color map. Next to the color map are three boxes, one each for hue, saturation, and value. Each box has a range of numerical values. The user first selects a color from the map, then instructs each of the boxes to modify that selection in hue, value, or saturation. The HSV mode requires learning to mix color in a way that is associated only with digital design. Unlike the CMYK or RGB modes, it does not correspond to either additive or subtractive color mixing.

Not all printed images produced digitally are created by a user mixing colors. A scanner takes artwork (a photographic transparency or piece of opaque art) and, using a special kind of lamp (5200 Kelvin), separates the colors into three electrical impulses, one each for red, green, and blue. Each electrical impulse is relative in strength to the quantity of that color in the art. The electrical impulses, which are analog information, are translated by the scanner into digital information (pixels) and printed in process colors directly onto paper. Digital cameras take pictures directly onto the hard drive, where they can be retrieved into RAM, worked on, and printed or saved on disks.

No matter what mode is used to mix colors on screen, digitally produced printed material is

References

limited to process color (CMYK) mixing. Programs, particularly RGB programs, are capable of displaying a greater range of colors on-screen than can be printed. Color images created for storage and distribution on disks are potentially richer in their color than any other medium of visual communication.

Hope, Augustine, and Margaret Walch. *The Color Compendium.* New York: Van Nostrand Reinhold Company, 1990.

Itten, Johannes. *The Art of Color,* trans. Ernst Van Haagen. New York: Van Nostrand Reinhold Company, 1961.

Endnotes

1 Johannes Itten, *The Art of Color,* trans. Ernst Van Haagen (New York: Van Nostrand Reinhold, 1961), p. 130.

2 Pantone, Inc.'s check-standard trademark for color reproduction.

3 A monochromatic color composition has only one hue, but it can have more than one level of value and/or saturation.

4 The color wheel, a term sometimes used for the artist's spectrum, is also used to mean a circle of color devised by scientist James Maxwell to demonstrate a psychophysical response called **persistence of vision** and the additive nature of colored light.

5 Not to be confused with the scientific concept of color temperature, which refers to the temperature in degrees Kelvin (K) of a piece of metal called a blackbody as it heats up and changes color.

6 **Brilliance** is sometimes used as a synonym for saturation, but brilliance in common usage also describes strong, clear tints.

7 Acknowledging the indignation that consumers have voiced when they have painted walls "white" only to see them as "pink" when green carpet is installed, paint manufacturers now provide charts showing which whites should be used with green schemes, blue schemes, orange schemes, and so on. The colors are formulated to prevent the surprises caused by simultaneous contrast.

8 See Tertiary Colors and Saturation, p. 125.

9 Also called process inks, or process blue, process yellow, and process red.

10 Different programs use this mode under different names: HSL (hue, saturation, lightness), HSB (hue, saturation, brightness).

Chapter 8

THE WRITTEN IMAGE

LANGUAGE AND WRITING / EAST AND WEST: THE EVOLUTION OF MODERN WRITING / PICTOGRAPH, IDEOGRAPH, AND PHONOGRAPH / PHONETIC SYMBOLS / ICONS / WRITING / PRINTING / TYPE / LETTER FORMS / WORDS / TEXT / TYPOGRAPHIC GRID / THE GREEKS HAD A WORD FOR IT

"Writing, in the widest sense, is everything—pictured, drawn, or arranged—that can be turned into a spoken account: everything, then, that can again be expressed or even thought in simple sounds or words."

Alexander Nesbitt[1]

Language is the communication or expression of ideas and feelings through the sounds of speech. Speakers of a common language are able to communicate very complicated and specific ideas between individuals. Words are always subject to some degree of interpretation, but language is inarguably the best means we have of conveying ideas, reasonably intact, from one human being to another.

Writing is a way to convey language without a voice. A written word is the visual form of a spoken word. Writing and art are equally visual communications: Either can record and preserve reports of events and people; either can describe, or instruct; either can convey emotion.

Art and design demand the active participation of both artist and observer. The artist creates an image that is in some way a message and the observer must decipher that image in order to find the message. Writing "tells" rather than suggests. Writing reduces the role of reader as interpreter and shifts the burden of communicating to the writer. It is essentially one-way communication. Written language is the translation of *telling* into a visual form. A **written image** is a planned arrangement of letters, words, and text that merges two potent forms of communication—design and writing—into a single entity.

The great majority of written languages derive from two ancient ones, Chinese and Greek.

Chinese writing was known to exist as early as 2900 B.C. Chinese is ideographic, (see pages 142–148) written vertically and read right to left. Chinese uses two kinds of figures: *wen,* which are simple figures to convey a single idea like "man," and compound figures called *tzu.* Tzu figures combine wen characters in different ways to impart compound ideas (Roman, 83). Only the complete design of a Chinese character gives information about the group of ideas to which it belongs. By A.D. 200 there were 10,000 Chinese characters; today there are about 500,000. Chinese writing, culturally isolated until the nineteenth century, has remained essentially unchanged for 3000 years. Chinese is monosyllabic and has no suffixes, prefixes, or accents. It is made of pictographic concepts (symbols or ideograms), except at those rare times when it may be used phonetically to translate a foreign word into the sounds of a Chinese language (Roman, 79–85) (See Figure 8-1).

Chinese writing became a basis for other Far Eastern written languages. Japanese and early Korean writing used the Chinese characters as a basis for written languages that were both ideographic and phonographic.

Japanese and Korean are polysyllabic, so basing polysyllabic written languages, with some phonetic elements, on the ideographic, monosyllabic Chinese characters required ingenuity. The difficulties involved led to a unique event in the history of written language.

Floating Archives Inc.

f
l
o
a
t
i
n
g

a r c h i v e s

Japanese needed 48 syllabic phonographs (phonograms) and Chinese was adapted to its sounds reasonably well, but Korean needed 1300 phonographs. In 1443 a new Korean writing was created from ideas that originated in India. The new written language was a phonetic, alphabetical writing, written vertically, the "only significant and successful attempt of this sort on a national scale in the history of writing."

Modified in the twentieth century to read horizontally, Korean is the only native phonetic written language of the Far East, and some scholars consider it a perfect phonetic system (The Korean Language, 1983, 105–17; Diringer, 443) (See Figure 8-2).

Greek is the source of the European written languages. Western Europeans use an alphabet that is very close to the Roman alphabet that

FIGURE 8-1.
Letters and words are elements of pure design.

grew from the original Greek; Eastern Europeans use the Cyrillic alphabet that grew from a Slavic one that came from the Greek.

The Greek alphabet developed in Asia Minor. Ancient Near Eastern languages were favorable to a syllabic system (Roman, 16). Cuneiform, the earliest known writing of Asia Minor (4000 B.C.) was both ideographic and phonetic. The phonetic written language of Asia Minor that led to the Roman and Cyrillic alphabets also led to Hebrew, Arabic, and the Brahmin writing of the Indian subcontinent. The Greeks had a full alphabet of 24 letters, and the name of its first two letters, *alpha* and *beta,* became the *word* for a complete alphabet.

Not all successful written languages survived over time. Egyptian hieroglyphs (sacred carvings), known to have existed as early as 3000 B.C. were still in use as late as A.D. 394. At least 29 of the more than 3000 known Egyptian characters were phonetic (Roman, 210–17, 257–59) and the Egyptians had more than one form of writing: one for sacred use, another for the business of daily life. The pictographic writing of Central America,[2] first known in the Mayan culture and emulated later by the Aztecs,[3] has been dated as early as 1000 to 700 B.C.[4] The Mayas had the first known numerals, including the concept of zero, but the isolation of Central America prevented their spread to any other culture. Runic writing (*runa* means secret, or mystery), an A.D. third- to sixth-century North German form, came from the Etruscan. These and other written languages, like Polynesian, flourished then vanished, remaining outside the development of modern writing (Roman, 269, 319) (See Figure 8-3).

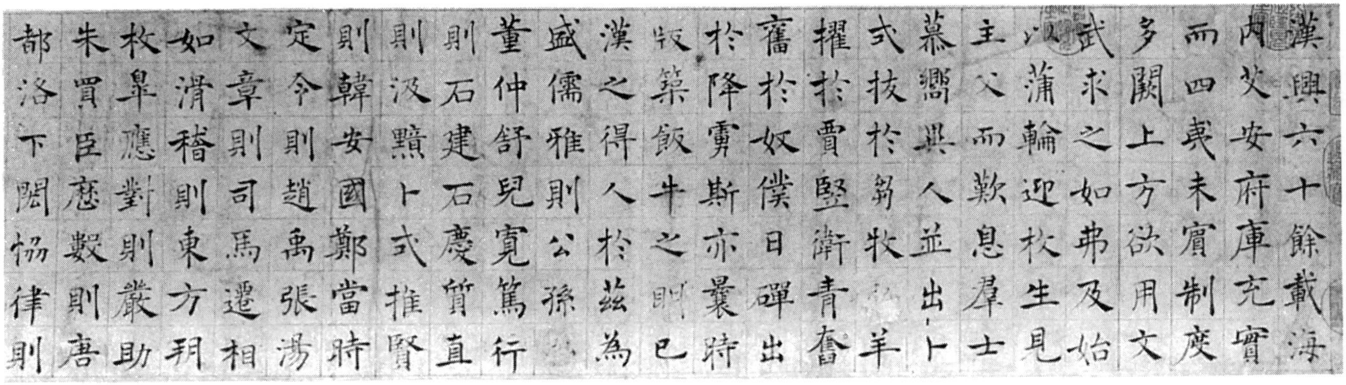
漢興六十餘載海內乂安府庫充實而四夷未賓制度多闕上方欲用文武求之如弗及始以蒲輪迎枚生見主父而歎息羣士慕嚮異人並出卜式拔於芻牧弘羊擢於賈豎衛青奮於奴僕日磾出於降虜斯亦曩時版築飯牛之朋已漢之得人於茲為盛儒雅則公孫弘董仲舒兒寬篤行則石建石慶質直則汲黯卜式推賢則韓安國鄭當時定令則趙禹張湯文章則司馬遷相如滑稽則東方朔枚皋應對則嚴助朱買臣歷數則唐都洛下閎協律則

FIGURE 8-2A. *Chinese writing has hundreds of thousands of individual characters, each representing a separate object or idea.*

Consonants

K, G	K
K as in King	CH as in Chemistry

N	D, T	T	L, R
N as in night	D as in dog	T as in top	L as in labor

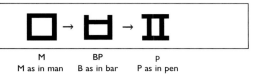

M	BP	P
M as in man	B as in bar	P as in pen

s, sh	CH, J	ch
S as in especially	J as in Jar	CH as in church

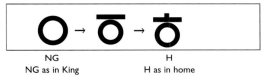

NG	H
NG as in King	H as in home

Vowels

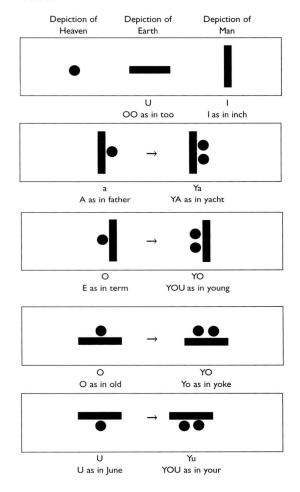

Depiction of Heaven	Depiction of Earth	Depiction of Man
	U	I
	OO as in too	I as in inch

a	Ya
A as in father	YA as in yacht

O	YO
E as in term	YOU as in young

O	YO
O as in old	Yo as in yoke

U	Yu
U as in June	YOU as in your

FIGURE 8-2B.

The Korean alphabet is phonetic, with consonants and vowels. Only five of the vowels are commonly used.

rabbit

water

dog

FIGURE 8-3.
Aztec is a lost written language. Only a few of the characters are understood today.

earthquake

rain

flower

Pictograph, Ideograph, and Phonograph

The earliest form of writing is the **pictograph,** an image that represents a whole word. Pictographs are pictorial representations of the objects they stand for. They have no relation to spoken language. A horse pictograph represents a horse; it is an idea that can be understood in any language, or by someone with no language at all. A prehistoric cave painting of a hunt is a composition of individual pictographs. The magical meaning of the painting can never be known, but the tale of the hunt and the identity of each animal in it is communicated unmistakably (See Figure 8-4).

Writing that developed from the pictograph took two parallel courses. The first was the substitution of symbols for pictographs—written symbols removed from the pictorial image. A symbol is understood only when its meaning is already known, and it depends on language for that understanding.

A parallel step in the development of writing was the **ideograph.** Ideographs are symbols that represent word-ideas like *love* or *anger* as well as word-objects like a *person* or *animal.* Pictographic and ideographic writing are visual forms of written language. They have no relation to the sounds of speech. Together they can communicate a complete language, but writing devised in this way requires literally thousands of individual characters. All writing has passed through, or stopped at, each of these stages (See Figure 8-5).

The next development in writing was the **phonograph** (or phonogram), a written symbol

FIGURE 8-5.
An ideograph represents an idea, like this computer icon for "system crash."

FIGURE 8-4. *Pictographs are the earliest writing. The stories they tell can be understood without a common language.*

that represents the sound syllables of a whole word or part of a word rather than representing a whole object or idea. Phonographs are a step between pictographs and phonetic letters. Phonographic symbols can be combined to make a word whose meaning is unrelated to the meaning of its parts. An imaginary symbol for the sound "man" combined with one for the sound "date" makes "mandate," a word with *sounds* identical to "man" and "date" but with no meaning associated with either. Many forms of writing still employ these elaborate symbols alone or in combination with ideographs (Roman, 418).

Phonetic symbols are marks that represent a sound of spoken language. Each symbol, called a **character** or **letter,** represents one sound or a small group of similar sounds. All the letters together constitute an **alphabet.** Additional sounds are represented by combined characters, like the sounds *sh, th, ch, ph.* Phonetic letters have advantages over other forms of writing. A limited number of letters can be used to represent all the sounds of speech, so phonetic alphabets are reasonably easy to learn. Languages grow and change over time, never faster than with present-day communication. Phonetic alphabets do not require new symbols for new words. If a word can be spoken, a spelling can be devised for it (See Figure 8-6).

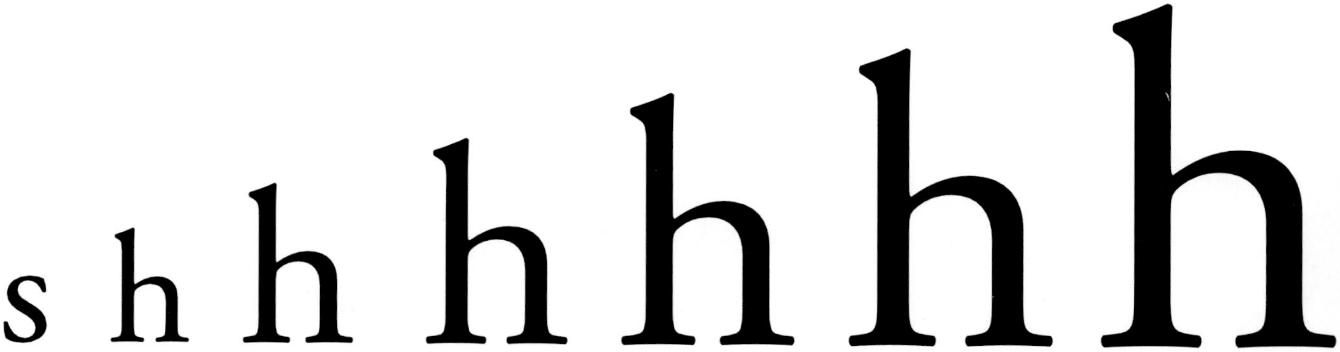

s h h h h h h

FIGURE 8-6.
Phonetic symbols
represent sounds.

Phonetic letters are characteristic of European written languages. European written languages also make use of ideographs, notably the Arabic numerals (1, 2, 3, etc.). Numerals are ideographic symbols that represent abstract ideas. Only Roman numerals (letters that represent numbers) were used in the West until the mid-tenth century. A Roman numeral requires the reader to make the distinction between its phonetic meaning and its ideographic meaning. By the mid-tenth century Arabic numerals were in general use in the West for mathematics, but Roman numerals continued to be used in charters and documents until the sixteenth century.[5] (Roman, 268). Today Roman numerals are used in design to imply timelessness and the permanence of antiquity (See Figure 8-7).

FIGURE 8-7.
Roman and Arabic numerals.

Icons

The icons of computer screen display are ideographs—symbols that represent software functions. A user **interfaces** (or "communicates") with a computer through written language. Information and instructions in digital design are given and received through visual commands. A phonetic alphabet is irrelevant for this human-computer encounter—computers do not have spoken language. New written languages have come into being whose entire purpose is as a means of access to computer functions (See Figure 8-8).

Mechanical languages are technical symbols used by manufacturers in encoding computers. Users of software are generally unaware of these languages, and when their characters are seen on the monitor they are perceived as bewildering marks.

Icons are the ideographic language of programs. Icons are symbols designed for nontechnical users. They represent access to programs and to program functions. An icon can symbolize a complete application ("click on ⟦Press here⟧ to enter program") or a function within it, like *draw, fill, cut, paste, expand, move, rotate, delete,* etc.

The design of icons is critical to the "user-friendliness" of a program. Type designers create variants of existing characters, but icon designers create wholly new ones. An average icon is about the size of a postage stamp. Within those parameters it must be readily identifiable with the function it represents. Pioneer icon designer Susan Kare calls icons "more like traffic signs than illustrations." Her designs, including the signature icons of the Macintosh, combine familiarity of form, simplicity, and humor.[6]

Whole words can become so closely identified with their typefaces that they become symbols (or icons) for their meaning. The script "Coca-Cola" is as unmistakable an icon as the block lettering of a traffic STOP sign.

FIGURE 8-8.
Computer icons are ideographs for functions.

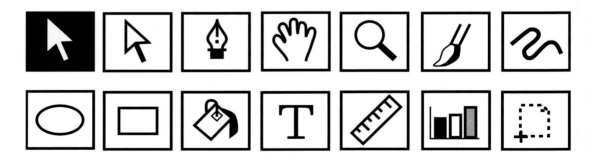

Writing

Writing is done by hand whether the writing tool is a pen, pencil, brush, or cursor. **Cursive writing** is handwriting in which words are formed by letters that are actually connected.[7] **Lettering**, also done by hand, is the planned arrangement of individual letters of any style to form words, sentences, lines, columns, and text.

Script is writing in which words are made up of unconnected letters whose design makes them appear to be connected. Script is a writing form between lettering and cursive writing (Roman, 333). **Calligraphy** is stylized and expertly handwritten script, an art form of writing that includes named styles as well as individual interpretations (See Figure 8-9).

FIGURE 8-9. *The beauty of the phrase "In the Name of the Benevolent and Forgiving God" is expressed in the beauty of Islamic calligraphy.*

Printing

Writing is an ideal medium for disseminating ideas, but the volume of material that can be produced by handwriting is small. **Printing** is a way of reproducing writing (and images) repeatedly. Printing appeared first in the Far East. Block printing, hand-carved wood blocks of whole pages with fixed letters, was known in Japan as early as A.D. 770: the first wood block-printed book was published in China in A.D. 868. By the early fourteenth century movable characters made of clay, wood, and tin had culminated in the Korean invention of bronze movable type (Carter, Day, Meggs, 30; Roman, 293). The printing technology of the East did not reach the West in any functional way. In Europe before the fifteenth century, handwriting was the only means of reproducing information.

Movable metal type was invented in the West by Johann Gutenberg (1400–68). His first book, a bible, appeared in 1456. The invention of movable type fulfilled a democratic function in the West. Before printing, the spread of ideas was limited to a religious and cultural elite. The greater population was illiterate. Ideas were spread through pictographic storytelling. Public works of art—frescoes, paintings, and posters—conveyed religious, social, and political ideas (See Figure 8-10). Printing made mass communication—and mass literacy—possible.

FIGURE 8-10.

The story of the Tower of Babel is communicated clearly even to those who cannot read.

For 500 years following the invention of movable type, printed material was the principal way in which ideas traveled. In the twentieth century television asserted the primacy of spoken words over written ones. Television reaches an enormous population. It has replaced reading as the principal medium of mass communication and diminished the role of writing in the spread of ideas. The emerging Information Superhighway (Internet and World Wide Web) as a means of mass communication signals a return of the importance of writing. *Most information in cyberspace is communicated visually through written words.*

Type, originally the block and raised letter that was inked for use in printing, has come to mean any printed character: a letter, number, or mark (like $, *, %).

A **typeface** (or **face**) is a specific design or style of type (See Figure 8-11). The letters and other characters of a typeface have similar characteristics of proportion, angle, stroke weight, and simplicity or elaborateness. A typeface typically includes uppercase and lowercase letters,[8] small capitals (the same size as the lowercase letters), numbers, and symbols like dollar signs. A **type family** is a related group of typefaces. Most typefaces are available as plain, bold, and italic versions. Many are available as other variants as well—ultrabold, condensed, outline, light, and so on (See Figure 8-12).

Type size is measured in points. A **point** is a standard measure of letter height (including a space above it) equal to about $1/72$ of an inch. A **pica** is 12 points, or roughly $1/6$ of an inch. Letters that are pica size and below are generally used for text; larger letters are used for headings (See Figure 8-13).

Typography, once the making up of printed material from movable type (or typesetting), now has the larger meaning of design composition done with type. **Typography** is the selection and use of type as a stylistic element in design no matter what method or means—from hand cutting to digital design—is used to produce it. When handwriting or handwritten letters are used as elements of design they are, with few exceptions, treated as art rather than as typography (See Figure 8-14).

Design

Design

Design

Design

𝘿𝙀𝙎𝙄𝙂𝙉

FIGURE 8-11. *Different ideas about the word* design *can be expressed by using different type styles.*

The big brown cow
The big brown cow
The big brown cow
The big brown cow
The big brown cow
The big brown cow
The big brown cow

FIGURE 8-12. *A type family is a single style of type in a selection of weights and angles.*

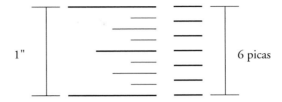

1"   6 picas

FIGURE 8-13. *Type size is measured in points. There are 12 points in one pica and six picas to one inch (or 72 points to one inch).*

FIGURE 8-14. *Typography is the selection of type as a stylistic element in design. The devastation of Chernobyl is conveyed by the ravaged letter forms.*

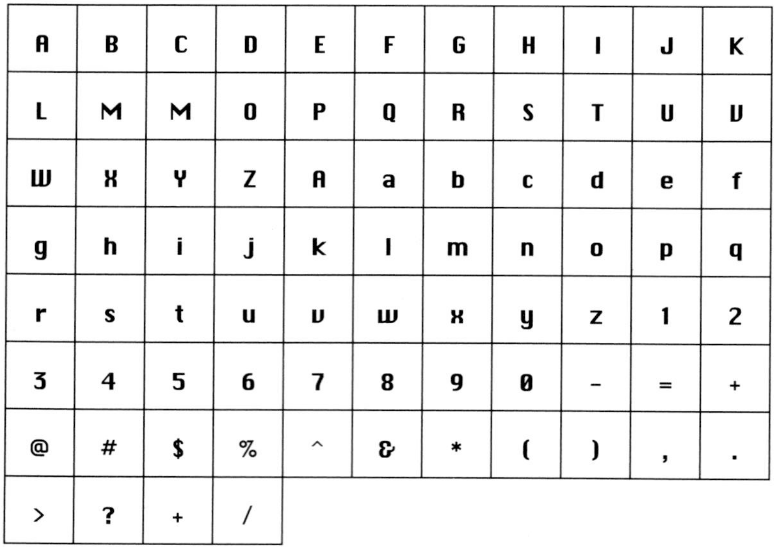

A	B	C	D	E	F	G	H	I	J	K
L	M	M	O	P	Q	R	S	T	U	V
W	X	Y	Z	A	a	b	c	d	e	f
g	h	i	j	k	l	m	n	o	p	q
r	s	t	u	v	w	x	y	z	1	2
3	4	5	6	7	8	9	0	-	=	+
@	#	$	%	^	&	*	(	)	,	.
>	?	+	/							

FIGURE 8-15. *A complete digital font.*

A **font** is a complete assortment of characters in a single size, weight, and face. A **digital font** is a font encoded in digital form and available to the user as software (See Figure 8-15). A good digital font can be printed to the highest resolution possible on the printer and looks good on the monitor screen at a resolution of approximately 72 dpi (dots per inch). Most important, a font must be scalable: It must be possible to rescale (change the size of) letters without losing the crispness of their edges. Vector-based (draw) programs are generally better suited to typography than pixel-based (paint) programs, which are software resolution-dependent for both printing and monitor image, and become jagged when rescaled (See Figure 8-16).

FIGURE 8-16. *Good typography demands that letters be scalable—sharp and legible in all sizes.*

Letter Forms

Letter forms evolved from the way each letter was first written. European alphabets have both straight and curved lines and include uppercase letters (capitals, or majuscules) and lowercase letters (minuscules). Roman letters (capitals) carved in stone were almost entirely rectilinear. The simple rounded letter form known as uncial lettering, seen as early as 300 B.C. was the natural result of writing in ink with a reed or quill. (Roman, 249, 404). Letters used today are descendants of these forms (See Figure 8-17).

Typefaces are characterized by their letter forms. Typefaces are broadly categorized as serif, sans serif, script (also called cursive), and novelty faces[9] (Carter, Day, Meggs, 32). Serif letters include a "tail" that originated as the chisel marks of Roman monumental lettering. Sans serif (literally, "without serif") faces developed from a simplified letter form originated by William Caslon in the early nineteenth century. Script faces have individual letters whose fluid lines make them appear to be connected when they are grouped into a word. They give the impression of cursive writing (See Figure 8-18). Novelty faces are a grab-bag of quirky or hard-to-categorize type styles (See Figure 8-19).

FIGURE 8-17. *Capital letters developed from Roman monument forms.*

FIGURE 8-18. *The letters of script type appear to be connected, like handwriting.*

FIGURE 8-19. *Novelty typefaces like this one are for special uses. They can be problematic when used for text and should be used with a heightened awareness of their legibility.*

LANGUAGE IS THE COMMUNICATION OR EXPRESSION OF IDEAS AND FEELINGS THROUGH THE SOUNDS OF SPEECH. SPEAKERS OF A COMMON LANGUAGE ARE ABLE TO CONVEY COMPLICATED AND VERY SPECIFIC IDEAS FROM ONE PERSON TO ANOTHER. WORDS ARE PERCEPTIONS. THEY ARE SUBJECT TO SOME DEGREE OF INDIVIDUAL INTERPRETATION, BUT LANGUAGE IS INARGUABLY THE BEST MEANS WE HAVE OF CONVEYING IDEAS, REASONABLY INTACT, FROM ONE HUMAN BEING TO ANOTHER.

Language is the communication or expression of ideas and feelings through the sounds of speech. Speakers of a common language are able to convey complicated and very specific ideas from one person to another. Words are perceptions. They are subject to some degree of individual interpretation, but language is inarguably the best means we have of conveying ideas, reasonably intact, from one human being to another.

FIGURE 8-20. *Which paragraph is easier to read? Note the similarity of size and shape of the upper case letters.*

A

B

FIGURE 8-21. *Serif (a) and sans serif (b) letters.*

A Serif

Language is the communication or expression of ideas and feelings through the sounds of speech. Speakers of a common language are able to convey complicated and very specific ideas from one person to another. Words are perceptions. They are subject to some degree of individual interpretation, but language is inarguably the best means we have of conveying ideas, reasonably intact, from one human being to another.

B Sans serif

Language is the communication or expression of ideas and feelings through the sounds of speech. Speakers of a common language are able to convey complicated and very specific ideas from one person to another. Words are perceptions. They are subject to some degree of individual interpretation, but language is inarguably the best means we have of conveying ideas, reasonably intact, from one human being to another.

The design of letters helps to determine whether words will be easy or difficult to read. A letter form must be familiar enough for recognition and, at the same time, different enough in shape and internal pattern to be distinguished easily from other letters. Highly stylized letters or letters that are very similar are difficult to read. Lowercase letters are more individual in shape than uppercase letters. The similarity of size, shape, and weight of capital letters makes them more difficult to tell apart than lowercase letters (See Figure 8-20).

Serif faces in general are more legible than sans serif styles. Each serif letter has a more individual shape than its sans serif counterpart. The thick and thin variations within each letter lend an impression of turning in space, so individual letters not only have different shapes but appear to occupy space in different ways (See Figure 8-21).

The final shape of a letter is a design product. Letters vary in size, scale, proportions, internal pattern, angle, and stroke weight. The first known type design from Italy in 1465 has been followed by hundreds of others, including typefaces created by William Morris, England's foremost designer of the Arts and Crafts Movement, and by Hector Guimard, the French avatar of Art Nouveau. By the late nineteenth century at least 50 different named typefaces were in ordinary use, many bearing the designer's name: Caslon, Baskerville, Goudy, Bodoni.

FIGURE 8-21.
Serif (a) and sans serif (b) text.

Words

Technology has a direct impact on design: The invention of the power loom changed textile design; the invention of precast concrete changed architecture. Digital design has changed the face of typography. No special equipment is now needed to originate a typeface. Since the late 1980s it has been possible for anyone with the appropriate software to originate a font, a revolution that has brought about an outpouring of new typefaces. Typefaces are now almost infinite in number, style, and name (including Holtzschue, designed as a gift to the author's daughter).

Individual letters are grouped into **blocks** to form words. A **word** is a Gestalt experience; understood as the larger, single, word-entity. A written word is a whole image. It is the visual form of the spoken word. A word is only secondly a group of separate sounds.

The understanding of words depends as much on spacing—between letters and between words—as it does on letter recognition. Written Latin text was not separated into words, sentences, or paragraphs until the ninth century and its continuous text (known as *scriptura continua*) is quite difficult to read. The opposite is also true—words formed by letters that are spaced too widely are difficult to read, as are words that are irregularly spaced (Roman, 405) (See Figure 8-22).

Language is the communication or expression of ideas and feelings through the sounds of speech. Speakers of a common language are able to convey complicated and very specific ideas from one person to another. Words are perceptions. They are subject to some degree of individual interpretation, but language is inarguably the best means we have of conveying ideas, reasonably intact, from one human being to another.

Word spacing

Language is the communication or expression of ideas and feelings through the sounds of speech. Speakers of a common language are able to convey complicated and very specific ideas from one person to another. Words are perceptions. They are sub-

Character spacing

Text

Words together form **text.** Text is the main body of written material. Text in design is treated as a block, or mass (See Figure 8-23), and is arranged with other elements of design, such as photographs or illustrations, in the typographic grid (See below). Text in graphic design is a form to be arranged on a page.

Text reads well when each word is separately and readily recognizable, yet also seems continuous with other words. In all writing—lettering, typography, calligraphy, or any other—it is typical for letters to align in some way. Chinese letters must be inscribed in a perfect (imaginary) square. The same is true for Arabic Kufic and Square Hebrew letters (Roman, 19, 84). Early Korean phonetic writing was in a square but changed later into freer forms (The Korean Language, 99). European letters align at their base. Letters (even those with ascending and descending elements) rest on an imaginary line (See Figure 8-24). That implied line helps to move the eye across the page. Margins are implied lines, cues that direct the eye to stop and start. Serifs may also serve as implied lines that connect letters, reinforcing the wholeness of each word-image, and increasing the apparent horizontal flow of words across a page. Script, with its impression of connected letters, is also thought to have superior legibility over sans serif faces.

Not all letter forms are chosen to facilitate the flow of words across a page. Some letter forms are selected to create word emphasis. An Internet message written in all capital letters is understood as "shouting."

Language is the communication or expression of ideas and feelings through the sounds of speech. Speakers of a common language are able to convey complicated and very specific ideas from one person to another. Words are perceptions. They are subject to some degree of individual interpretation, but language is inarguably the best means we have of conveying ideas, reasonably intact, from one human being to another.	Language is the communication or expression of ideas and feelings through the sounds of speech. Speakers of a common language are able to convey complicated and very specific ideas from one person to another. Words are perceptions. They are subject to some degree of individual interpretation, but language is inarguably the best means we have of conveying ideas, reasonably intact, from one human being to another.	Language is the communication or expression of ideas and feelings through the sounds of speech. Speakers of a common language are able to convey complicated and very specific ideas from one person to another. Words are perceptions. They are subject to some degree of individual interpretation, but language is inarguably the best means we have of conveying ideas, reasonably intact, from one human being to another.	Language is the communication or expression of ideas and feelings through the sounds of speech. Speakers of a common language are able to convey complicated and very specific ideas from one person to another. Words are perceptions. They are subject to some degree of individual interpretation, but language is inarguably the best means we have of conveying ideas, reasonably intact, from one human being to another.

FIGURE 8-23. *Text in design is treated as a block with value (relative light or dark). Space between lines is called* leading. *Tight leading makes the text block appear darker, and open leading makes the text block appear lighter.*

Axjd

ascender
cap height

x-height

baseline

descender

Aaxjd

ascender
cap height

x-height

baseline

descender

FIGURE 8-24.
*European letters align
at their base except
for round forms,
which are treated to
read correctly rather
than to measure cor-
rectly. They dip below
and above the base
and the x-height.*

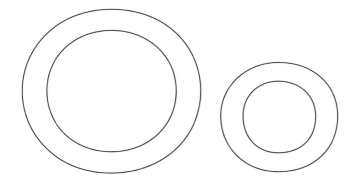

Typographic Grid

A **typographic grid** provides a framework for page design. It is a modular, two-dimensional grid that employs the X (vertical) and Y (horizontal) axes of Cartesian coordinate space. The grid creates an underlying foundation for page design and promotes continuity in a publication even when individual pages have apparently different configurations. The typographic grid uses a rectangular or square module within which the relative areas of text, image, margins, and columns are manipulated (See Figure 8-25A–C).

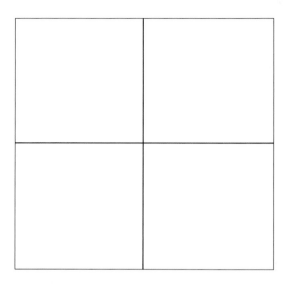

Language is the communication or expression of ideas and feelings through the sounds of speech. Speakers of a common language are able to convey complicated and very specific ideas from one person to another. Words are perceptions. They are subject to some degree of individual interpretation, but language is inarguably the best means we have of conveying ideas, reasonably intact, from one human being to another. Language is the communication or expression of ideas and feelings through the

Language is the communication or expression of ideas and feelings through the sounds of speech. Speakers of a common language are able to convey complicated and very specific ideas from one person to another. Words are perceptions. They are subject to some degree of individual interpretation, but language is inarguably the best means we have of conveying ideas, reasonably intact, from one human being to another. Language is the communication or expression of ideas and feelings through the

A

Language is the communication or
expression of ideas and feelings through
the sounds of speech. Speakers of a common language are able to convey complicated and very specific ideas from one
person to another. Words are perceptions. They are subject to some degree of
individual interpretation, but language is
inarguably the best means we have of
conveying ideas, reasonably intact, from
one human being to another.Language

Language is the communication or expression of ideas and feelings through the
sounds of speech. Speakers of a common
language are able to convey complicated
and very specific ideas from one person to
another. Words are perceptions. They are
subject to some degree of individual interpretation, but language is inarguably the
best means we have of conveying ideas,
reasonably intact, from one human being
to another.Language is the communica-

Language is the communication or
expression of ideas and feelings through

the sounds of speech. Speakers of a com-

mon language are able to convey com-

plicated and very specific ideas from one

person to another. Words are percep-

Language is the communication or expression of ideas and feelings through the sounds of speech. Speakers of a common language are able to convey complicated and very specific ideas from one person to another. Words are percep-

FIGURE 8-25A–C.

The typographic grid is a framework for the arrangement of text.

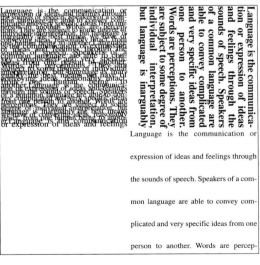

B

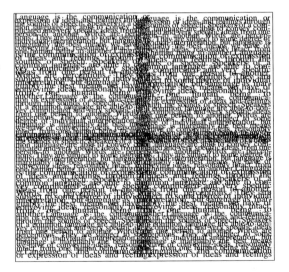

C

The Greeks Had a Word for It

Graphein is the Greek root of the English word *graphic*. *Graphein* means both writing and drawing (Roman, 417). Although "graphic arts" is widely used to mean design produced for printed material, it also refers to any piece of work produced by drawing or writing tools (pens, pencils, etc.), and printing devices, whether handprinted or mechanically printed. In graphic art, drawings and letters are equal (See Figure 8-27).

Letters and characters have always been elements of design. "Illuminated" letters (decorative initial capitals) embellished medieval manuscripts. The Chinese associated writing with aesthetics so thoroughly that "the form of a Chinese character, the way it is made, is an artistic rendering of the thought it conveys" (Roman, 80–85). Georges Braque made the first use of letters as elements of pure design (without language meaning) in 1913 (UNESCO, 48); artists now use letters, words, and text freely as pure forms without textual meaning (See Figures 8-26 and 8-28). Graffiti is—controversially—the communication design of the streets, merging images, letters, and expressive power.

Letters, words, blocks of text, and pages exist first as compositions and second as communications. The relationships of letters and words, lines, columns, margins and text, page, and pub-

FIGURE 8-27. *Hand-cut letters convey the name and style of an artist.*

Figure 8-26.
*Marilyn needs no
words!*

Yes, I said, I am overdone by you.
I want to be with you.
Your hands are large.
I want them resting. Voice
resting in my ear. Settling
The top of me agonizes
My dream, exquisite;
all of us in an open
area with a sky watching
the ordained one
tell us about standing
on our hands
–how the cranials loosen
allowing for weight. She,
so small and dark into a tour
causing me to gasp and exclaim

resurrection

What a beautiful tour!
My fantasy
The entire time I being lifted
by simply a thought of her
I seem to be falling in love. Out
of control I do not care
for other's feelings or decorum
because this feels good.
I do not want to be sanctioned.
I look forward to dreaming where
her gestures win.
Her voice rumbles.
And her large hands. This,
I know, is nothing to take lightly. OING IT." ❦ "THEY WERE

IT MADE ALL OF US LAUGH AS WELL, EVEN THOUGH WE HAD

FIGURE 8-28.
The digital font of this typographical layout has been manipulated to create unique characters.

lication are metaphors for the ascending complexities of graphic design composition. At each level there can be variations in size, scale, and proportion; color, texture, and value. Each element can be arranged in infinite numbers of ways. The style of letters and the words they make up is like emotional expression in vocal sounds. Digital design affords the graphic designer unparalleled speed, control, and freedom in composing a visual display of language.

References

Carter, Rob, Ben Day, and Philip Meggs. *Typographic Design: Form and Communication.* 2nd ed. New York: Van Nostrand Reinhold, 1993.

Diringer, David. *The Alphabet.* London: Hutchinsons Scientific and Technical Publications, n.d.

The International Communication Foundation. *The Korean Language.* Seoul: Si-Sa-Yong-O-Sa Publishers, Inc. and The Internationsal Communications Foundation, 1983.

Roman, Klara G. *Encyclopedia of the Written Word.* New York: F. Ungar, 1968.

UNESCO. *The Art of Writing.* Paris, France: UNESCO, 1965.

Endnotes

1 Nesbitt, Alexander, *The History and Technique of Lettering* (New York: Dover Publications, Inc., 1957), p. 3.

2 Natives of North America had no written language at all, only mnemonic (memory-aiding) devices for chronology and accounts.

3 Mayan writing dates from at least 1000 B.C. and is ideographic, very little translated. The Aztec language is thought to have developed as ideas taken from the Mayan, but with a few phonetic characters that approximate sounds. More Aztec has been deciphered than Mayan.

4 UNESCO, *The Art of Writing* (Paris, France: UNESCO, 1965), p. 24, puts it at 700 B.C.; Roman (259) puts it at 1000 B.C.

5 Called "Arabic," but actually originating in India and introduced to Europe by the Arabs.

6 *New York Times,* 26 August 1996, sec. D5. Zuckerman, Laurence. "*The Designer Who Made the Mac Smile.*"

7 **Cursive** comes from the Latin word for running or flowing, a common root for the cursor, the moving indicator of digital design and the flowing style of cursive writing.

8 The terms **lowercase** and **uppercase** came into use from the locations of the boxes in which printers kept their movable type—larger letters in the upper box, smaller ones in the lower.

9 The historical categories of type (chronologically) are Old Style, Italic, Transitional, Modern, Egyptian, Sans Serif, and Novelty.

WORKBOOK

Getting Started

Only by drawing do we really learn to see. It is critical that drawing be done from life. Drawing from photographs, fantasy, or from other pictorial resources does not train the eye, the hand, or the mind. A good drawing does not have to be perfectly rendered to tell a story. It can be interpreted in many ways and accomplished with almost any tool or medium, but it needs to be observed from life.

The exercises in this section are meant to be done in a variety of media, including a computer. Most digital design today is done on a Macintosh computer, and a great proportion of popular design software is meant for use on one or more versions of the Mac. The speed of technological change and competitiveness of the computer industry suggests that no platform be advanced over others. If you have access to a computer, many of the exercises below can be accomplished using it. If you do not have access to a computer, the exercises can be accomplished using traditional media.

Keep a sketchbook. The sketchbook is meant to be carried at all times (so it is obviously not a venue for the computer). The sketchbook is not just for drawing; it is a place to gather information—written, taped, drawn, and painted. Like the computer memory, the sketchbook is meant to record, store, and provide information.

Begin (and continue) a collection of small, odd bits—yarns, textile fragments, pebbles, interesting sticks, small objects, color papers, interesting samples of text, shells, sparkles, metal, wood and plastic oddments—anything that has interest and is potentially part of a design composition.

A surprising number of the exercises below involve research and writing. They are critical for developing an ability to think in design problem-solving ways.

Comfort, Safety, and Success

Work in good illumination—in natural light whenever possible. Some sketches may be done under conditions of low light, but these are special circumstances. Glare-free light is important. If natural light is not available, a combination of incandescent and fluorescent light works well. Art and architectural suppliers sell a clip-on desk lamp with this double-light source combination.

Rest your eyes by alternating exercises or activities. The ability to see declines with eye fatigue and the direct light of a monitor screen is particularly tiring.

Work in well-ventilated, draft-free areas. Be aware that substances like rubber cement and some markers have heavy and potentially dangerous fumes. Do not work near anyone who is smoking or near an open flame (like the pilot light of a gas range).

Keep working surfaces clean and free from old dried paints, chalk dust, pencil residue, food remnants, oils, or other contaminants. A protective drawing table pad (similar to one used by architects) can be rolled out on any table and provides a good surface (it can also be rolled and carried to class). Clean the working surface regularly with any powder or liquid abrasive cleaner and wipe free of grit with clean water.

Be careful not to contaminate any food with art materials. Although federal laws now make hazardous colorants more an exception than a rule, there are still plenty of materials out there that will cause illness if (accidentally) ingested.

If you are using a computer, keep it clean. Special cleaners are available for all (cleanable) parts of the computer, but the keyboard pads or mouse can be cleaned carefully with a Q-tip moistened (not dripping) with a liquid household cleaner. *Never allow liquids to get into any computer part!*

Paper absorbs the natural skin oils from your hand, causing it to repel paint, pencil, inks, and even chalks. Protect paper and finished work by using a piece of clean paper under your working hand. Tracing paper works well for this. The paper will also protect against some accidental spills or spattering.

Materials

Every student should keep the materials below on hand at all times:

- **Sketchbook:** small enough to carry at all times, large enough to record observations and thoughts.

- **Brushes:** Winsor and Newton series #233, or Robert Simmons White Sable: sizes 4 and 6, and old or cheap brushes for mixing. For serious work, the Winsor and Newton series 7 sable are expensive but wonderful.

- **Portable work surface:** If a clean surface is not reliably available, get a drafting table protector or large sheet of inexpensive white paper to use as a surface.

- **Roll of white tracing paper.**

- **Small covered jars for storing mixed paint.** The plastic containers used by take-out restaurants are ideal.

- **Small peel-off labels and a fine-point permanent marker or a china marker.**

- **Ceramic or disposable paint mixing trays.**

- **Containers for water, one at least 1 quart.**

- **Cork-backed steel ruler at least 18″.**

- **X-Acto knife (recommended) and plenty of extra blades.**

- **Self-healing cutting board:** at least 12 × 15″.

- **Selection of triangles:** one right triangle at least 12″ and one 30/60/90.

- **Compass and protractor.**

- **Inexpensive paper:** for quick sketching.

- **A selection of papers:** in different weights, colors, and textures.

- **Drawing pencils:** a range from 2H to 6B.

- **Eraser:** kneaded or other.

- **Rubber cement, rubber cement thinner, and a rubber cement pickup.**

- **Drafting tape or drafting dots.**

- **Selection of markers:** in different values of gray and sepia.

- **Water-based paints:** gouache, watercolors or other.

And, of course, a computer with a good supply of floppies for archiving work!

Exercises

Exercise Series I

1. What are some differences between manmade beauty and natural beauty? Sketch two examples of each.

2. What differences are there between an experience of beauty that is transient (like a symphony) and one that is permanent (like a statue?)

    List as many examples of transient beauty as you can.

    Using only color and form without representational images, illustrate three experiences of transient beauty.

3. Give as many examples as possible of tools that require human skill and might be used to create works of art or design. What skills are needed for each tool? Example: A typewriter: finger control, coordination, speed.

4. Give an example of a tool you consider obsolete because of new technologies.

    Identify a tool that you think will soon be obsolete because of new technologies.

    Identify a tool that may be considered a passing phase or fad.

    Identify a tool that your think will be important in the future.

    Did you base your choices on fact or personal opinion?

5. What are the key differences between art and design?

    What functions does each serve?

    What functions do both serve?

6. Give an example of great art and explain the reasons for your selection.

    Give one example of "bad" art and explain the reasons for your selection.

    Give one example of "great design" and describe the specific attributes that make it great.

    Give one example of "bad design" and describe the specific attributes that make it bad.

7. Find one example of something that is (or was at one time) considered beautiful by one culture and distasteful by another. Example: Bound feet.

8. Find an example of an outrageous statement of aesthetic principle: Example: The opinion of the color blue, in Chapter 1, page 9.

9. Find examples of design that convey emotion visually, rather than by narrative content. Look for cues such as strong contrast, intense color, or diagonal lines.

    Are any of these examples indicative of a particular historical art movement or style?

10. Find examples of British or American art used as propaganda.

Exercise Series II

1. Describe ways in which the computer has changed the way you think.

2. Look in the Help Wanted section of a local newspaper and identify the computer skills that relate to a field that interests you.

3. Identify two analog media. Can they can be translated to digital information?

4. If you own or have access to a computer:
   What platform are you working on?
   How much RAM and hard drive space is available?
   Identify the software that is installed and how much RAM is required to run each program.
   Identify and list all external devices that are connected to the computer.
   What is the bit-depth of your monitor?
   How many colors can your monitor display?

5. Select a paint program and open up an image. What change, if any, occurs if the bit-depth of the monitor is changed?

6. Identify pixel-based software in your computer.

7. Identify vector-based software in your computer.

8. Pixel-based images do not enlarge well. Why not?

9. Would vector- or pixel-based software work best to produce a clean circle (without "jaggies")? Which type of software would be better for working with a photo collage?

10. Research the differences between a draw program, a layout program, and a word processing program by listing the specific programs and their functions.

11. If a scanner is available, compare the file size (memory) of a black-and-white (grayscale) photograph scanned at 72, 150, and 300 dpi.
    When would you need to scan images at 72 dpi?
    Why would you need to scan images at 300 dpi?

12. Describe ways in which the World Wide Web (WWW) can serve as a design resource. What other functions can the Web serve?

13. Find as many examples as you can of computer use in art and design disciplines. Select one of these pieces. Investigate the platform, software, and time involved in creating it.

> Do you believe that the computer hinders or enhances the experiences of creating art and designs? Why?
>
> Do you think the computer will replace all/most traditional ways of creating art and designs? Why?
>
> What is the difference between a technician and an artist/designer?
>
> Does an artist/designer also need to be a technician? If yes, what ratio of skills would you expect this person to have? Example: Design skills 90 percent, technical skills 10 percent.

14. Do you think the computer hinders or enhances the process the making good design?

> Do you think the computer should be used for everything?

15. Presentations in corporate America are typically made with slides, large charts, and graphs. Describe ways that presentations can be made using a computer (other than having a group of people standing in front of a monitor). Use technology magazines and technology programs on television to help start identifying new concepts.

16. In corporate America, communication is typically conducted on paper or with a telephone. List other ways people are communicating.

Exercise Series III

1. Give three visual examples that make you feel threatened.

> Give three visual examples that make you feel pleasure.

2. List things that come to mind when you think of: sight, sound, smell, taste, touch. Example: Sight—sun, colors; Sound—music, noise; Smell—chocolate, bacon, lilies.

3. Create five compositions, one for each sense. Collect images from magazines that relate to each sense. Do not use words. Rip the images from the magazines (do not cut them) and make a collage that completely covers an 8 × 10″ board. Try not to repeat images in the collage (i.e., don't show only eyes, noses, ears, tongues, and fingers).

4. Repeat the project in #3 above using only color fields and drawn lines to represent each sense. Think about how the colors and lines of each composition attempt to communicate to the viewer. Example: Concentrate on what a lemon tastes like and identify the physical experience, then convey it in colors.

5. Draw or gather as many reproductions of symbols as possible.

      Categorize these symbols as:

            Words/letters only

            Symbolic use of color

            Symbols as images

            Symbols as simple shapes

      Identify the meaning for each symbol and how or what it communicates.

6. Collect from magazines as many swatches as possible of reds, violets, blues, greens, oranges, and yellows. When colors are difficult to categorize, make an arbitrary decision by asking yourself what the color "feels" like. Using ALL the colors, make a collage that completely covers a 12 × 15" board.

7. Using color pencils and fast gesture movements draw three different light environments from life. Example: A neon diner sign at night, a traffic signal with the sky behind it, or your room at night with a television as the only light source. Place colors with free, overlapping gesture lines.

8. Design and construct a free-standing structure at least three feet tall and made of paper. Develop three separate drawings of this construction using wash ink. Each drawing should represent illumination from a different direction: from behind, inside, and in front of your structure.

9. List as many natural and manmade light sources as you can.

10. Observe the effect of at least four different light sources on two different materials, like fabric and paint or plastic laminate and carpet, which appear to be the same color. Compare them to each other under fluorescent light, incandescent light, daylight, and halogen light. Describe what you see.

Exercise Series IV

1. Using cut black paper, black gouache paint, opaque black ink, or a computer, illustrate any image or figure using black line on white paper.

      Repeat the figure, using only mass without line. The mass must be solid. Do not outline.

2. Using *Bartlett's Familiar Quotations* or any source of your choice, select a quotation that you feel best expresses or defines the essential meaning of the word *form*. Cite author, work, and date for the quotation. Be prepared to discuss the reasons for your selection. *Do <u>not</u> select "Form follows function."*

3. Draw a room environment using only points. Place the points in key areas where corners meet or at the edges of planes. The product of the drawing should be a freckled composition. Connect lines in your point drawing to see how accurately you have placed the points.

4. Draw the same room environment with only vertical lines. Place the lines on the page to correspond to the actual places where vertical lines are seen. No lines will touch; all lines go in the same direction. Connect the vertical lines with horizontal ones to see how accurate your placement is.

5. Draw yourself from head to toe in front of a full length mirror. Do not just focus on the plane of the mirror alone. Look at the area surrounding the mirror and objects reflected in the mirror. Fill up the page.

6. Select a newspaper or magazine photograph. Turn the photograph sideways or upside down. Lay tracing paper over it. Using heavy marker and vertical lines only, blacken the dark areas of the photograph. Do not follow the contours of the image. Omit light areas. Do not attempt to illustrate light or middle grays. Reverse the image so that it is right side up. What does the result tell you about image?

7. Find and sketch two doorways: one illustrating small scale, and one illustrating grand or monumental scale. Include a human figure in each sketch. Use any medium.

8. Select a conventional figure (animal or structure). Illustrate it in appropriate proportions.
    Illustrate the same figure a second time with distorted proportions.
    Using any book, shelter publication, special color section newspaper, or periodical, identify an object, or architectural interior or exterior that illustrates proportions distorted from the traditional or expected.

9. Illustrate any figure or scene using line only, between 3 × 5″ and 5 × 7″. The illustration should be realistic: an animal, person, scene, or still life. Starting with your line drawing, work out three levels of abstraction from individual shape to pure form. There will be a total of three illustrations.

10. Make a contour drawing of a walnut, using hard line. Try to get every detail.
    Repeat, using a heavier hard line.
    Repeat, using charcoal.
    Do the same exercise with an apple or banana.

Exercise Series V

1. Using any mixed media, create a model of a home for intelligent ants of the twenty-third century. Suggested materials: clay, foamcore board, balsa, paper, sticks, rocks. Use at least three textures for the surface of your ant home. Observe the effect of a light source that is positioned directly above the textured surfaces. Move the light source so that the light reaches the surface at increasingly sharp angles. Describe what you see.

2. Using cut paper, gouache paint, opaque inks, or a computer, create a single design composition with blocks of black, white, and one gray. Do not use line.

    Incorporate your entire first design into a new, larger composition.

3. Using geometric forms in torn paper, create a design with more than one vertical axis.

4. Using geometric forms in cut paper, illustrate more than one form of alignment in a single composition.

5. Use paint, marker, or the computer to create a single figure. Render it in black, white, and one gray. Use blocks or masses only (no line).

    Reduce OR enlarge the figure.

    Repeat it in a random design over an area 8 × 10″.

    Reduce OR enlarge the figure.

    Repeat it in a geometric design over an area 8 × 10″.

6. Using any source, bring in (mounted) five or more different materials as close as possible in color and as different as possible in texture. Examples of materials: stone, straw, plastics, ceramic material, laminates, textiles, wallcovering, metal, wood, yarn.

7. Draw a small composition using line, mass, and/or texture. Cover the entire surface. Place it in a square border.

    Repeat, placing your design completely within a round border.

    Repeat, placing your design completely within a border drawn to Golden Section proportions.

8. Draw an object no larger than 12″ high.

    Repeat the object, making a symmetrical design.

    Repeat the symmetrical design, creating a radial symmetry.

9. Create a design using black and white only, in which the ground is not clearly defined (like a zebra's stripes).

10. Select and identify by location, date, and architect any twentieth-century structure of architectural interest or merit. You may use the interior or exterior of the structure. Make a copy of the illustration. Example: The entrance to the Louvre in Paris, designed by I.M. Pei c.1990.

Select and identify by location, date, and architect (where possible) a second structure from any period from Ancient Egypt to A.D. 1800 that has characteristics in common with your first selection. Make a copy of the illustration. Example: The Great Pyramid at Gizeh.

Describe and compare the two in terms of their form, size, scale, proportions, use, orientation in the landscape (exposure, if interior), axes, surface materials, and surface embellishment. Note: A good starting place is *A History of Architecture* by Sir Banister Fletcher (London: Butterworths, 1987).

Exercise Series VI

1. Locate a beginning book on perspective drawing (there are dozens of good ones).

Draw a box in one-point perspective.

Draw a box in two-point perspective.

Draw a hallway in one-point perspective.

Redraw the hallway, changing the position of your horizon line.

2. Measure a room and draw it as a series of elevations in a scale of ½″ = 1′. Do not try to show perspective. Include all possible dimensions: length and width of room, ceiling height (ceiling heights, if more than one), window openings, width of door and window frames, width or height of panel moldings, picture moldings, crown moldings, locations and dimensions of heating and air conditioning elements and electrical switches, receptacles, and fixtures.

Make as many drawings as you feel you must to illustrate a maximum of information. Include only permanent elements of the room—do not include cabinets, draperies, furnishings, carpets, or anything else that is removable.

3. Find a public space and a private space. Describe each space and compare the two in terms of size, scale, proportion, contrast of form, color and surface, continuity within the composition, and static or dynamic impression.

4. Find a sacred space and sketch it in any medium. Describe your emotional response to it. What design factors have helped to create this emotional response? Design a sacred place of your own.

5. Select a small object and illuminate it from directly above. Sketch, showing shadow.

Move the light at least twice, repeating the drawing.

6. Make a series of drawings of the same subject in which each drawing has an added depth cue. Begin with relative height, add overlap, shading and shadow, and color.

7. Go to see a hologram. Describe your response to it. Were you fooled into thinking it was reality? Why or why not?

8. Using mixed media (paper, yarn, odd bits), create a static composition.
   Repeat, making a dynamic composition.

9. Using the computer or any paint in pointillist technique (dots of color so tiny that they form an optical mix) and only saturated colors, illustrate any continuous rounded form (like an apple or pear).

10. Locate (in a museum or book) a fourteenth-century attempt at perspective drawing. List the pictorial depth cues employed by the artist.
    Locate (in a museum or book) a nineteenth-century American trompe l'oeil painting. List the pictorial depth cues employed by the artist.

Exercise Series VII

1. Create a simple, outlined coloring book-type of design on white paper. Make three copies of the design. Using gouache paint, illustrate the design:
   (a) Monochromatically.
   (b) Using complementary colors.
   (c) Using analogous colors.

2. Write a one-page typed essay describing the color palette of any historical period. Discuss influences on that palette. (Recommended sources: Color Compendium, Color Source Book, books on arts and crafts, textiles, or design for the given historical period). Use at least two reference books. On a board no larger than 12 × 15" and using commercial paint color samples and fabric swatches ONLY, present a palette of colors suitable for a contemporary interior that is inspired by colors of the historical period you chose.

3. Using commercial paint chips, select a single, cool, saturated hue and six steps of value in that hue (total of seven chips). Include both tints and shades.
   Repeat, using a warm color.

4. Select ONE publication (newspaper or magazine). Use as many issues as you need for the assignment. Glossy magazines work best. Do not mix publications. Cut or tear black-and-white photo fragments from the magazine. Arrange them in an overlapping collage, from darkest to lightest, on a sheet of paper at least 8 × 10″. What areas were the hardest to select?

5. Using any sources, bring in (mounted) a color scheme for a public shelter that will give the residents a sense of home rather than a sense of institution. Include at least eight samples. Select your scheme from ONE of the following kinds of color groupings:

    (a) Monochromatic.

    (b) Complementary.

    (c) Analogous.

6. Obtain a sample of screen-printed wallpaper. The more colors (screens) in the paper, the better. Select from the commercial paint chips colors to match, as closely as possible, the colors in the wallpaper.

7. Select the strongest possible red or red-orange paint and paint a circle approximately 3″ in diameter in the center of a white paper at least 9″ square (or cut one out of red paper and mount in the center of a white paper). Place a small black dot, about ⅛″, in the center of the red circle. On a second sheet of white paper, the same size, place an ⅛″ black dot in the center.

    Stare at the red circle without blinking as long as possible. Blink once and transfer your eyes to the black dot in the center of the blank white paper. What do you see? Why?

    Select the strongest possible yellow paint. Paint a geometric design of diamonds or circles, each about 2″ at the widest point in the center of a sheet of white paper 9″ square. There will be four wide and four high, with a slight border of white. The diamonds or circles should just touch. Have ready a second sheet of white paper the same size, blank. Stare at the yellow design without blinking as long as possible. Blink once and transfer your eyes to the blank white paper. What do you see? Why?

8. Using commercial paint samples ONLY, choose at least seven colors that are harmonious. Include an appropriate "white" and a tertiary dark in the group. Either at the beginning of your collecting or when the group is complete, choose an appropriate theme and NAME the collection. NAME each individual hue within the collection. Arrange your colors as if for professional presentation on a board no larger than 9 × 12″.

9. Find examples of additive mixtures. Illustrate them in a wet medium (ink, paint).

10. Create a simple, outlined coloring book-type of design on white paper. Make two copies of the design. Using gouache paints, illustrate the design twice in the same hues: first as fully saturated colors and then in muted colors.

Exercise Series VIII

1. Locate four letter forms that are at least 72 point. Draft each character in pencil, making it exactly as it appears but at least 10″ tall and/or wide. The letters should be filled (not outlined).

2. Make photocopies of your letters. Cut each into four parts. Make a two-dimensional composition using the parts.

3. Select one of the original 72-point letter forms that you have reproduced. Create a twenty-seventh letter for the alphabet with similar characteristics of font or style.

4. Find a typeface that expresses your personality and a second one that is totally uncharacteristic of your personality. Design two separate business cards using these faces.

5. Gather writings that have been produced by you, your family, or your friends. Using a layout program and a printer, design and illustrate a small catalog of the writing.

6. Design a poster for a Shakespeare play. Use no images.

7. Select two books, two magazines, and one newspaper. Photocopy one page from each. Try to identify the grid on which each was designed. Indicate the grid on your photocopy (use color for the grid).

8. Find a public area that would benefit from an information kiosk. Select and photograph a site for the kiosk. Draw it in elevation. Plan the signage for "information." Make a sales presentation showing how the design would fit into the site. Include human figures cut from magazines to illustrate activity around the kiosk.

9. Write, in one paragraph, directions from your house to a friend's house.
     Using these instructions, design a map that does not use words or representational images. Use only points, lines, planes, and forms.

10. Design a series of computer icons for the seven deadly sins: lust, greed, gluttony, envy, anger, pride, and sloth.

GLOSSARY

A

ABSOLUTE COORDINATES See **world coordinates.**

ABSTRACTION The reduction of a person, animal, or object to its simplest, most essential form without individual identity.

ACHROMATIC Having no discernible hue or color.

ACTIVE WINDOW A currently selected window, where the next command will be applied. The active window is always on top of overlapping windows.

ACUITY The ability of the eye to see detail.

ADDITIVE MIXTURE Color seen as a result of light only.

ADDITIVE PRIMARIES Wavelengths of light which must be present to yield white light: red, blue, and green.

ADMIXTURE In painting, the addition of a single hue to all or most colors in a composition.

AESTHETIC Concerning the sense of beauty, as in "an aesthetic judgement."

AESTHETICS A branch of philosophy dealing with ideas of beauty in order to establish the meaning and validity of works of art; also, rules and principles of beauty that are considered valid for a particular time and place.

AFTERIMAGE A mirage or false image generated by the eye in response to stimulation by a single color in the absence of its complement. Also called *successive contrast.*

ALERT BOX A box that pops up on screen (announced by beeps) to give information or a warning. Alert boxes don't require input, but they sometimes require an action. Also called a *message box.*

ALGORITHM A procedure for solving a problem.

ALIGNMENT The relationship of the edge or corner of one design component to another; also, the relationship of the center line of one design component to center line of another.

ANALOG DATA (INFORMATION) Information stored as continuous data, as it is experienced.

ANALOGOUS COLORS Colors adjacent on the spectrum, sometimes defined as hues, limited to the range between a primary and secondary. A group of colors including two primaries but never the third.

ANTI-ALIASING A technique for smoothing the appearance of the rough edges of bit-mapped graphics, usually by blurring their edges.

APPLICATION A synonym for software or program. Common application types include word processing, spreadsheets, database managers, modelling and graphics programs. Most programs are called applications, unless they are utilities or system software.

AREA The measurable surface of a two-dimensional plane or three-dimensional figure (solid).

ART Human skill; a visual communication of images, ideas, or feelings; or the tangible products of art.

ARTICULATION A joining or juncture of individual parts; connectedness.

ARTIST'S SPECTRUM The full range of visible hues in subtractive color: red, orange, yellow, green, blue, and violet; expandable to include any and all hues in between them. A synonym of color circle.

ASCII Acronym for the American Standard Code for Information Interchange. It is a system for referring to letters, numbers, and common symbols by code numbers (A is 65, for example). This widely used file format is useful for transferring files between different computers, like Macs and PCs. On the Mac, ASCII files are often called text files. Pronounced "as-key."

AXIS A sensed rather than perceived center of a plane or volume; an imaginary center line.

B

BACKING UP Copying some or all of the files on the hard drive to different disks (like floppy disks) so that stored data will not be lost if the original versions are damaged, lost, or stolen. The copied files are called backups.

BALANCE Unlike components of equal or similar strength creating a visual equilibrium. Balance is intuitive rather than measurable. See **symmetry.**

BALLOON HELP A Help feature in some software that pops up cartoonlike, message balloons with explanations. It is turned on or off from the Help menu.

BBS Acronym for Bulletin Board Service. BBS is a noncommercial service usually run by a user group or software company. Messages can be exchanged with other users and software downloaded or uploaded by dialing a BBS, using a modem. A BBS has fewer features than commercial on-line services, but it is usually free except for the phone call.

BÉZIER CURVE A curve used in draw programs that consists of mathematically defined line segments connected by control (anchor) points. Complex curves can be created by manipulating the anchor points.

BEZOLD EFFECT An effect in which all colors in a composition appear lighter by the addition of light outline, or darker by the addition of dark outline; or an effect in which a background appears lighter because it carries a linear design in light line, or darker because it carries a linear design in dark line.

BIT The smallest piece of digitally coded information. A bit is either on or off.

BIT-MAP An image on the monitor made up of pixels (or dots) that correspond exactly to the information in memory. In pixel-based (paint) programs the artist has control over each individual pixel.

BIT-MAPPED FONT A font in which each character is made up of a pattern of dots. A bit-mapped font requires a separate set of character maps for each size of type (10 point, 12 point, and so on) for correct display. Also called a *fixed-size* or *screen font*. Compare to **OUTLINE FONT.**

BIT-MAPPED GRAPHIC   An image made up of dots (bits); typical of paint, image-editing, and 3-D graphics programs. Sometimes called a raster image. Compare to **OBJECT-ORIENTED GRAPHIC.**

BOMB   Another word for *crash*. In some platforms bombs are heralded by an alert box with a picture of a bomb. Compare to **CRASH** and **HANG.**

BOOTING   Starting up a computer, which loads the system software into memory. Restarting the computer is called rebooting or a warm boot.

BORDER   Lines or edges that enclose a composition and define what is within and what is outside it; an arbitrary device for establishing the limits of a design.

BRILLIANCE   The combined qualities of highlight reflectance and strong hue, typically found in saturated colors and strong tints.

BUG   A mistake, or unexpected occurrence, in a piece of software (less commonly, in a piece of hardware). Bugs cause the computer to hang or crash.

BYTE   A collection of 8 bits, or 256 possible variants of *on* or *off*.

C

CALLIGRAPHY   In Europe, a form of handwriting that originated in the Medieval period. Calligraphy is an art practiced in many written languages; it has been called the art and manner of writing with beauty and grace.

CARRIED COLORS   Colors in an image or design which are laid on the background. See **ground.**

CARTESIAN COORDINATE SPACE   See **world coordinate space.**

CD-ROM   Acronym for Compact Disc, Read-Only Memory. A type of storage device that looks like an audio CD and stores as much data as a large hard disk. It is a popular means of distributing fonts, photos, electronic encyclopedias, games, and multimedia offerings. Files on a CD-ROM can only be read. They cannot be changed, added to, or deleted.

CHROMA   Color, or its presence. Used commonly as a synonym for saturation. See **saturation** and **maximum chroma.**

CHROMATIC   Having hue or color.

CLICKING   Pressing and immediately releasing the mouse button. To "click on" something is to position the pointer over its icon on the screen and then click.

CLIPBOARD   A temporary storage area in memory that holds data last cut or copied. The pasting function inserts its contents into a document. Some programs have a menu item that displays what is on the clipboard.

COLOR   A category of visual experience including hue, value, and saturation. Also, a synonym for hue; the name of a color. See **hue.**

COLOR WHEEL   A term for a circle of color devised by scientist James Maxwell to demonstrate a psychophysical response called *persistence of vision and the additive nature of colored light.*

COLORANT   A substance that reacts with light by absorbing some wavelengths and reflecting others, giving an object or surface its hue. Also called *color agent.*

COLORWAY   A specific combination of colors for a product (textile, wall covering, or other) available in more than one combination of colors, as "This paisley is available in a red colorway, a green colorway, and a gray colorway."

COMPLEMENTS; COMPLEMENTARY COLORS Colors directly opposite on the artist's spectrum or color circle. Every pair of complements contains the three primary colors (red, yellow, and blue) in some proportion or mixture.

COMPOSITION   A complete entity, something meant to be sensed as a whole. Composition includes the idea of arrangement, or relative placement, of elements within the whole. Also, a putting together, a grouping of ingredients and the manner of their combination. The word *design* is often used alone to mean design composition. Composition may be fluid or rigid, studied or accidental. Intricate compositions are constructed of smaller ones. Compositions may be two- or three-dimensional.

CONFIGURATION   The relationship between forms: another way to characterize composition.

CONTINUITY   Ideas, forms, colors, or styles that serve to connect design components within a single extended composition; as in architecture and interior design when forms, colors or style connect rooms or spaces within a single project.

CONTRAST   Two (or more) independent components or ideas of form, color, or style that together form one complete idea or composition but serve separately to reinforce and emphasize each other's differences.

CONTRAST REVERSAL   A variation of afterimage in which the "ghost" image is seen as negative of the original image and as its complementary color.

COPY PROTECTION   Any of the various strategies that companies employ to prevent the unauthorized (and illegal) copying of their software.

CPU   Acronym for Central Processing Unit, the brains of the computer. The CPU interprets and executes the actual processing of data.

CRASH   A problem (often caused by a bug) that causes a program (or the entire operating system) to stop working unexpectedly. If a program crashes it can sometimes be recovered with a command. More often, it will need to be rebooted. See also **bomb** and **hang.**

CURSIVE WRITING   Writing in which letters are connected or flow together (from *cursus,* meaning a "running" or "course"). Most often used to describe handwriting, but also to characterize typefaces that appear to run together.

CURSOR   A moving marker or pointer on the monitor screen that is used to indicate locations so that command functions can be utilized.

D

DEFAULT   An optional choice in software that will be used unless it is deliberately changed. It often refers to preset parameters such as the margins in a word processor or the volume in a sound control panel.

DEMOTIC WRITING   Writing used by the people, rather than by priests (from *demos,* meaning "the common people"). Egyptian demotic writing, like hieratic writing, ultimately included both pictographic and phonographic symbols.

DEPTH   A dimension downward or inward; used to describe the vertical plane of an interior volume like a swimming pool (downward) or a desk drawer (inward).

DESIGN   Art fused with function in an object that will be produced in multiples by others; also the act of originating applied art.

DESIGN CONCEPT   A broad solution to a design problem without resolution of details.

DESIGN PROCESS   Procedure for solving design problems.

DESKTOP   What is seen on screen when in the finder: the menu bar, the background pattern,

trash icon, disk icons, files, folders, and so forth. A computer metaphor for home base.

DESKTOP PUBLISHING   The process of designing printed documents (brochures, newsletters, magazines, books, etc.), often done using a page layout program on a computer.

DIALOG BOX   A box that appears on the screen (often after a command has been issued) and requests information or a decision.

DIGITAL INFORMATION/DATA   Data stored in small discrete samples.

DIGITIZE   To turn something from the real (analog) world into digital data on a computer. A scanner digitizes pictures or text, a soundboard records music or a human voice, a videoboard inputs video from a VCR or camcorder.

DILUTION   Changing a pure or saturated hue by lightening, darkening, or muting (or by the addition of black, white, gray, or its complement).

DIMENSION   A measurement in a single direction.

DISK   A thin round platter on which computer data is stored in either magnetic or optical form. The disk is circular but its case is usually rectangular. The main types are floppy disks, hard disks, and CD-ROMs.

DOCUMENT   The file that is created and modified using an application. Examples are a letter or a drawing.

DOS Acronym for Disk Operating System, refers to MS-DOS or PC-DOS, disk operating systems used on IBM personal computers, and compatible machines. Pronounced "dahss."

DOWNLOAD To receive information from a remote computer and store it.

DRAG To move the pointer (cursor) while holding down the mouse button. Dragging can move an object, select an area indicated by a selection rectangle, or move down a menu.

DRAW PROGRAM A vector-based application for drawing solid objects and planes.

DRIVE A motorized device that reads information from, and writes information onto, disks or tapes. The main types are floppy disk drives and hard disk drives, but there are also drives for CD-ROMs, removable media, and tape.

DYE A colorant which is fully dissolved in a vehicle such as water or other liquid; a colorant in solution. Traditionally dyes were organic, but modern colorants are less rigidly categorized.

DYNAMIC Characterized by energy, action, or movement. Dynamic art and design has a sense or illusion of movement in stationary planes or masses. See also **kinetic art.**

E

E-MAIL Electronic mail; private messages sent between users of different computers, via a modem connection to an on-line service or BBS.

EMBELLISHMENT Decoration or beautification of the surface of a two- or three-dimensional surface. Embellishment is independent of form.

EPS Acronym for Encapsulated Postscript, a standard file format for high-resolution illustrations and images.

EQUILIBRIUM In design, a state of rest or balance resulting from the equal action of opposing forces.

EQUILIBRIUM In color perception, an involuntary, physiological state of rest sought by the eye. Equilibrium occurs when all three (additive or subtractive) primary colors are present within the field of vision.

F

FACE A specific design or style of type character.

FIBONACCI SERIES A numerical idea about ideal proportion presented as a series of consecutive numbers. Each number is the sum of the two preceding: 1, 2, 3, 5, 8, 13, 21, 34, 55, and so on. Any adjacent pair in the series is theoretically an aesthetically pleasing relationship when applied to a two-dimensional figure (or all three dimensions applied to the proportions of a solid).

FIELD In carpet and flag design, the term for the background upon which colors are laid. See **ground.**

FILE FORMAT The structure that the data for a particular document is stored in. Most applications can save documents in one or more standard formats as well as their native format. See also **native.**

FINDER   The basic program that generates the desktop and allows access and management of files and disks.

FLOPPY DISK   A 3.5-inch removable flexible disk (usually protected by a hard plastic case). Also called a **diskette.** Compare to **hard disk.**

FOLDER   A grouping of files.

FONT   A complete assortment of printing types of a single size and face (style or design). In computer terms, the software that creates a typeface.

FONT FAMILY   A group of typefaces designed to work together. A typical family has four members: regular, bold, italic, and bold italic.

FORM   The essential or abstraction of a figure; the arrangement of parts that differentiates one object from another without individual identity: the whole idea.

FORMATTING   In word processing, all the information beyond plain text belongs to a document. It includes character styles, spacing, indents, tabs, tables, and so forth. Also, another term for initializing a disk.

FUGITIVE   Easily fading or deteriorating color, usually used in reference to colorants.

FULL COLOR   See **saturated color.**

G

GAMUT   The full range of colors available in software and seen as the light display of a color monitor.

GIGABYTE   A measure of computer memory, disk space, and similar storage venues that is equal to 1024 megabytes (1,073,741,824 bytes). Sometimes a gigabyte is treated as an even billion bytes (**GIGA** means billion), but that's almost 74 million bytes short. Abbreviated as G, GB, or gig.

GLOSS   A highly polished, light-reflective surface quality.

GOLDEN SECTION   Also Golden Mean. An idea about proportion, frequently illustrated as a line with three points, A, B, and C. The relationship of A-B to B-C is identical to the relationship B-C to A-C; a proportional relationship of 1:616.

GRADIENT   A gradual increase or decrease of same visual quality like lightness, color, or texture, made up of intervals so close that individual steps cannot be discriminated.

GRAYSCALE   Anything that contains intervals of gray as well as black and white, such as a grayscale monitor, which usually displays 256 grays.

GROUND   The background against which colors, forms, or shapes are laid.

H

HANG   A crash where the computer ignores input from the mouse and keyboard. Also called a *freeze.*

HARD DRIVE   A rigid, sometimes removable, storage disk, and/or the drive that houses it. Hard disks usually have several disks and they store much more data (and it can be accessed more quickly) than data stored on floppy disks. Also called a *hard disk.*

HARDWARE   The parts of your computer that you can bump into: physical components such as hard disks, printers, modems, scanners, cards, keyboards, mice, and the computer itself.

HARMONY   A pleasing effect. In color, the pleasing joint effect of two or more colors.

HEIGHT   The vertical dimension or measurement of a plane or solid, top to bottom.

HIERARCHICAL MENU   A menu that has submenus attached to it.

HIERATIC WRITING   Writing used by priests. Used most commonly in reference to writing (other than carving) done by priests in ancient Egypt. See **demotic writing.** Hieratic writing, like demotic and hieroglyphic writing, ultimately included both pictographic and phonographic symbols.

HIEROGLYPH   A carved symbol used to represent a word, syllable, or sound. *Hiero,* meaning sacred or holy, used by priests; and *glyph,* meaning carved, incised, or raised. See also **demotic writing** and **hieratic writing.**

HIGH-DENSITY DISK   A floppy disk that can store 1.4 MB of data.

HIGHLIGHT   To make something stand out from its background. In screen display, it is used to show a file or function that it is selected or active. Highlighting can be done by reversing colors (for example, switching black and white) or, in the case of text, by placing a transparent colored bar over the words.

HUE   The name of the color: red, orange, yellow, green, blue, or violet.

HUE INTENSITY   The saturation or purity of a color its vivid-versus-dull quality. See **saturation.**

I

I-BEAM   The shape the pointer (cursor) normally takes when it is dealing with text. The I-beam is used to create an insertion point or to highlight text. Also called a *text tool.*

ICON   A picture, image, or other representation; a pictograph or ideograph. A computer icon can represent a file, folder, disk, or tool.

IDEOGRAPH   A written symbol representing an object or idea without representing its sounds. Also, a symbol representing an idea rather than a word.

ILLUMINANT MODE OF VISION   Color seen as light; viewer and light source only.

IMAGE   A representation or depiction of a person, animal, or object; also a form or shape seen against a ground. Images can vary from photographic likenesses to nonrepresentational forms that do not portray objects or natural appearances.

IMAGE EDITING   The use of a computer to modify an image.

IMPORT To bring data into a document from another document, often data that has been generated by a different application. For instance, text and graphics can be imported into a page layout program. Data sharing is made possible by an application's support of common file formats.

INCIDENT BEAM The beam of light emitted by a light source.

INITIALIZING Setting up a disk (any kind) to receive information. When a disk is initialized, its magnetic media is divided into tracks and sectors, and a directory and desktop file are created. Also called *formatting*.

INSERTION POINT The place in a document or dialog box where the next keystroke will add or delete text. The insertion point is represented by a blinking vertical line and is placed by clicking with the I-beam pointer.

INTENSITY Sometimes used as a synonym for brilliance, the strength of a hue. See **hue intensity** and **light intensity.**

INTERACTIVE Said of software (particularly multimedia) that gives the user some control over the way in which information is retrieved.

INTERMEDIATE COLOR(S) Colors on the spectrum between primaries and secondaries.

INTERNET A worldwide network that links thousands of individual networks and on-line services. Access to the Internet and its millions of users and thousands of news groups, databases, and directories is possible for users whose computers are connected through an Internet on-line service provider.

INTERVAL A visually equidistant step of sensation; a series of even steps of change or transition in form, color, size, surface, repeat, or other element.

K

KERN To adjust space between two characters.

KEYBOARD A means of computer input.

KEYBOARD SHORTCUT A combination of keystrokes that executes a command without choosing it from a menu. Also called *quick-key command.*

KILOBYTE A measure of computer memory, disk space, document size, and the like; equal to 1024 bytes. Abbreviated as K.

KINESIS Actual movement of parts.

KINETIC ART Art with actual moving parts, like the mobiles of Alexander Calder.

L

LAMP The correct term for a light bulb.

LASER PRINTER A printer that creates images by drawing them on a metal drum with a concentrated beam of light called a laser. An ink powder (called toner) sticks to the imaged portion of the drum and is transferred and fused to the paper, as with a photocopying machine.

LE MODULOR   A series of mathematically calculated dimensions, based on theoretically ideal proportions of the human body, as devised by Le Corbusier.

LENGTH   The longer of the two dimensions of a surface or plane, also the longest of the three dimensions of a three-dimensional solid.

LIGHT   Visible energy.

LIGHT INTENSITY   The light-reflecting quality of a color. See also **luminosity** and **value.**

LIMIT   The visual edge of a composition, the place where it stops.

LINE   In theory, a series of connected points in a single plane and single dimension; in design practice, a directional mass having length but little or no width.

LOAD   To get something ready to use on the computer.

LOCK   A function that prevents a file or disk from being changed. Locked data is also called *write-protected.*

LOG ON   To establish a connection to a network, on-line server, or BBS, usually by entering a user name (or identification number) and a password. Disconnecting is called logging off.

LUMINOSITY   Literally, light emitted without heat. Used to describe the light-reflecting quality of a color. Luminous colors reflect light, nonluminous colors absorb light.

M

MAJUSCULE   A capital letter. In majuscule printing all letters are of equal height.

MARQUEE   A rectangle of moving dots that surrounds a selected area in some programs.

MASS   In two-dimensional design, an expanse, tone, or color that defines form and is not specific or individual. In three-dimensional design, a solid that has or gives the impression of weight, density, and bulk.

MATTE   A smooth but dull, unpolished surface quality that diffuses light evenly.

MAXIMUM CHROMA   The strongest possible manifestation of a hue.

MEDIUM   A liquid, paste, viscous, solid, or other vehicle (substance) into which pigments or dyes have been introduced to form a transferable colorant such as paint, dye, crayon, or other.

MEGABYTE   A measure of computer memory, disk space, application size, and the like that's equal to 1024 K (1,048,576 bytes). Abbreviated as MB or meg.

MEMORY   The electronic storage medium (chips) where the computer stores system software, programs, and data.

MENU   A list of command functions.

MENU BAR   A horizontal strip across the top of the screen that contains the menu commands.

METAMERIC PAIR   Two objects that appear to match under one set of light conditions but do not match under a different set of light conditions.

METAMERISM   The phenomenon which occurs when two objects which appear to match under one set of light conditions do not match under another set of light conditions.

MINUSCULE   A small letter. Minuscule letters have ascenders and descenders.

MODEM   A piece of hardware that enables computers to communicate over telephone lines (each must also have a communications program). The modem translates digital data back and forth between computers as sounds carried over the phone lines. Modem is a contraction of *modulator* and *demodulator.*

MONITOR   The hardware that contains the display screen. A monitor is also called a *display* or *CRT.*

MONOCHROMATIC   Containing one hue only.

MONOTONE   Color without variation. Generally used to describe two or more colors of close or identical value and saturation.

MOTIF   A single, specific design element; an isolated and individual idea, form, or shape.

MOUSE   The standard hand device for positioning a cursor or pointer on screen. Moving the mouse causes the on-screen pointer to move in the same direction.

MULTIMEDIA   Any presentation or program that combines several media, such as graphics, sound, video, animation, and/or text. Multimedia is used as business presentations, CD-ROM games, educational software, and training systems. Multimedia programs are often interactive.

N

NANOSECOND   A billionth of a second. Used to measure the speed of memory (RAM) chips, among other things. Abbreviated as ns.

NATIVE   A term for *software* that is written specifically to run on a particular platform. Some native software can be run in emulation mode (slower) on a different platform. A native *file* is the format in which an application normally saves its documents. The native format is generally readable only by that application, although other programs can sometimes translate it using filters.

NEGATIVE SPACE   The area of a two-dimensional composition that is not occupied by motif or image. Negative space is often, but by no means always, the ground of a composition.

NETWORK   A group of computers set up to communicate with one another. A network can be a small system physically connected by cables (a Local Area Network, or LAN), or separate networks connected together to form larger networks (called Wide Area Networks, or WANs).

The Internet, for example, is made up of thousands of individual networks.

O

OBJECT MODE OF VISION The presence of a viewer, light source, and object.

OBJECT-ORIENTED GRAPHIC An image created by vector-based software.

ON-LINE Actively connected to other computers or devices. A computer is on-line when it is logged on to a network, BBS, or on-line service. A device such as a printer is on-line when it's turned on and accessible to the computer. It can also refer to software: an on-line help system can be called up in software, as opposed to opening a manual.

ON-LINE SERVICE A commercial service that (for a price) provides services such as e-mail, discussion forums, technical support, software libraries, news, weather reports, stock prices, plane reservations, and even electronic shopping malls. A modem is needed to access an on-line service.

OPPOSITION Elements of equal visual strength creating a balance of thrust or visual force.

OPTICAL MIX A new color which is seen as a result of the close juxtaposition of small areas of two or more other colors.

OUTLINE FONT A font in which the shape of each character is stored as a mathematically plotted outline that can be scaled to any size with no loss of quality and will print at the highest available resolution. Also called a *scalable font*.

P

PAGE LAYOUT PROGRAM Software designed to combine text and graphics, giving extensive control over design and typography. The cornerstone of desktop publishing.

PAINT PROGRAM Software that allows the user to create a digital painting and save the results as bit-mapped graphics. Compare to **DRAW PROGRAM** and **IMAGE-EDITING PROGRAM.**

PALETTE Literally, a board or plate upon which colors are mixed. Used to describe a group of colors used characteristically by an individual artist or designer, or in a specific design, group of designs or body of work. Also, the color display of an application seen on the monitor screen.

Also, a floating window within an application that sits above open documents so contents can be accessed easily. The palette can contain tools, buttons, colors, styles, or whatever is appropriate to the program.

PASTE To insert something into a document from the clipboard by choosing Paste from the Edit menu.

PASTEL An apparel industry term for colors diluted by white to high or middle value; clean tints with little or no muted quality.

PATTERN A design composition formed by the reoccurrence of components or motifs. Pattern may be geometric or fluid, regular or random.

PHONETIC SYMBOL   A picture or letter representing a sound of speech.

PHONOGRAPH   Picture symbols that represent syllables rather than whole words or ideas. Phonographs are a step between pictographs and phonetic letters. Combined phonographic symbols create complex words. Japanese writing employs these in part.

PHYSICAL SPECTRUM   The full range of visible colors of light as postulated by Newton: red, orange, yellow, green, blue, indigo (blue-violet), and violet.

PICA   A size of type (12-point), about ⅙ inch.

PICT   A standard file format for graphic files. It can contain both object-oriented (draw- or vector-based) and paint (pixel-based, bit-mapped) graphics and is the standard format for graphics that are cut or copied to the clipboard.

PICTOGRAPH   A symbol that is a pictorial representation of an object, showing the object in an identifiable way.

PICTORIAL SPACE   A sensed extension of the picture plane into depth.

PIGMENT   A colorant which is finely ground and suspended as minute particles in a vehicle. Traditionally, pigments were inorganic (earth colors), but modern chemistry has blurred this definition. Pigments, in general, are opaque.

PIRACY   Copying commercial software without permission and without paying for it; also called *theft*, *thieving*, or *skullduggery*.

PIXEL   One of the points of light that make up the picture on a computer (or TV) screen. The name is short for Picture ("Pix") Element. The more pixels in a given area—that is, the smaller and closer together they are—the higher the screen resolution.

PIXEL-BASED SOFTWARE   Software in which the entire screen image is held in memory and corresponds exactly to the image on the screen. Pixel-based images are also called *raster images*.

PLANE   An area of two-dimensional surface, determinate (fixed), extension (size), and spatial direction (position in space).

PLATFORM   A particular type of computer running a particular operating system. For example: the Mac, a PC running Windows, a PC running DOS, and a UNIX machine.

PLUG-IN   Software that adds capabilities to an application. An addition to an existing program; new features.

POINT   In type, originally a unit measure for type bodies in printing, equal to about 1/72 of an inch. Now used as a measure of type size.

POINT   In design, an imaginary location denoting position alone, covering no area.

POINTER   A little icon that moves on the screen when the mouse is moved. The most common pointer shapes are the arrow and the I-beam.

POP-UP MENU   A menu, typically found in a dialog box or palette, that pops up (or down, or to the side) when a pointer is clicked on its title.

PRIMARY COLORS　The simplest colors of the artist's spectrum; those that cannot be reduced or broken down into component colors: red, yellow, and blue. See also **additive primaries** and **process colors.**

PRINTER　A device that takes text and graphics sent from the hard drive memory or RAM and prints them onto paper. Most printers are computers in their own right, with CPUs and memory. Printer types include laser, inkjet, dot-matrix, thermal-fusion, dye-sublimation, and imagesetters.

PROCESS COLORS　Yellow, cyan (blue-green), and magenta (red-violet) colorants that, when mixed or laid over one another result in nearly all possible colors on the printed page. Used, with the addition of black, in four-color printing.

PROCESS PRIMARIES　Cyan (blue-green), magenta (red-violet), and yellow. See **process colors.**

PROCESSOR　The chip that contains the computer brains, or CPU. Sometimes called a *microprocessor.*

PROGRAM　A synonym for software.

PROPORTION　The internal relationship of the parts of one thing to each other.

PROTOCOL　A set of standardized rules for exchanging information between computers over a network or modem connection. For example, AppleTalk is a networking protocol, and Zmodem is a file-transfer protocol used in telecommunications. Protocols generally specify the data format, timing, sequencing, and error checking of data transmissions.

PUBLIC DOMAIN SOFTWARE　Software that has no copyright or fee, which means it can be copied, used, and even altered and sold. Also called *shareware.*

PULL-DOWN MENU　The kind of menu found on a menu bar. It pops down when the pointer is clicked on its title.

PURE COLOR　See **maximum chroma** and **saturated color.**

Q

QUITTING　To exit a program.

R

RAM　Acronym for Random Access Memory, where the computer holds system software, programs, and data that are currently in use. It is formally called Dynamic RAM (DRAM) because it is volatile—that is, the contents that have not been saved to the hard drive are lost when the computer is turned off or crashes.

RASTER IMAGE　See **pixel-based software.**

REFLECTED BEAM　The beam of light reaching an object which is reflected back to the eye.

RELIEF　Design area that projects into three dimensions from a two-dimensional plane but is not independent of it. Relief may be very slight (low relief) or close to fully round (high relief).

RENDERING The process of drawing a final image. In some graphic programs (such as 3-D graphics) it includes applying colors, textures, shadows, movement, and so forth, and outputting the image at a specified resolution.

REPEAT Regularly spaced vertical, horizontal, or diagonal reoccurrence of a motif or design composition.

REPETITION The planned, uninterrupted, and regular recurrence of a design element with a maximum of sameness; strongly related to structure.

RESOLUTION The sharpness and clarity of an image on screen or on paper, and how much detail can be seen. It is usually determined by the number of dots (pixels) per square inch—the more there are, the higher the resolution. Resolution is used to describe printers, monitors, and scanners.

RHYTHM Visual movement that can be established by repetition but also by forms and objects separated in space. Unlike repetitive elements, rhythmic elements may be interrupted.

ROM Acronym for Read-Only Memory; permanent computer memory that cannot be altered.

ROTATION A change in direction of a two- or three-dimensional mass without a change in form.

S

SATURATED COLOR The most intense manifestation of a color imaginable, the "reddest" red or "bluest" blue. Saturated colors are undiluted by black, white, or gray. Synonyms are pure color, full color, or hues at maximum chroma.

SATURATION The degree of purity of a color, its hue intensity, or vivid quality as opposed to muted or dull quality. A fully saturated color can contain one or two of the primary colors but never the third. Saturated color does not contain any black, white, or gray.

SAVE To transfer information (usually a document) from RAM to a hard drive or disc for storage.

SCALE The size of one thing relative to another, different thing; a relationship of comparison.

SCANNER A device that converts images (such as photographs) into digital form so that they can be stored and manipulated on computers. When used in conjunction with OCR (Optical Character Reader) software, a scanner can convert a page of text into an editable document.

SCREEN FONT Another name for a bit-mapped font.

SCREENSAVER A utility that temporarily replaces the current screen image with a blank screen or an amusing moving image. It's designed to prevent a static image from being permanently burned into the phosphors that coat the inside of the screen.

SCROLL BAR A rectangular strip that appears

on the right and/or bottom edges of a window when there is more information available than is currently displayed.

SECONDARY COLORS   Colors made up of two primary colors. In subtractive mixtures orange (red and yellow), green (blue and yellow), violet (red and blue); in additive mixtures cyan (blue and green), yellow (red and green), and magenta (blue and red).

SERIF   The fine-line "tails" of letters in certain typefaces, originating from the end chisel marks in stone cutting.

SERVER   A computer that provides shared, centralized resources—such as files, e-mail, modems, and printers—to other computers on the network. *Server* can also refer to the software that runs on such a computer.

SHADE   A pure color made darker, or with black added.

SHAPE   A form with individual identity.

SIMULTANEOUS CONTRAST   A spontaneous color effect resulting from a physiological response of the eye to stimulation by one color only. The eye, seeking equilibrium (presence of all three primaries in the field of vision), generates the missing primary or primaries.

SINGLE INTERVAL   The smallest difference between samples that a viewer can distinguish, established by the individual's threshold. See **interval** and **threshold.**

SIZE   The absolute measurement of a two- or three-dimensional form.

SOFTWARE   The instructions that tell a computer what to do. Also called *programs* or *applications.*

SOLID   Having three dimensions. See **mass.** Also having the mass or interior filled up.

SPECTRAL REFLECTANCE CURVE   The characteristic pattern of relative energy emitted by a specific lamp at the various wavelengths.

SPECTRUM   The full range of visible hues. See **artist's spectrum** and **physical spectrum.**

SPREADING EFFECT   See **Bezold effect.**

STATIC   Fixed, stationary, showing no movement.

STORAGE   Any medium that can store files, including a hard disk, floppy disk, or removable cartridge.

STYLE   A pattern of similar characteristics common to an object and others like it.

SUBTRACTIVE MIXTURE   Colors seen as the result of the absorption of light; the colors of objects.

SUBTRACTIVE PRIMARIES   The primary colors of perceived objects; the artist's primaries: red, yellow, and blue.

SURFACE   The outermost layer of a two- or three-dimensional thing; its "face" or "skin."

SURGE PROTECTOR   A device that protects computer equipment and data from being damaged or lost by variations in electrical current.

SYMMETRY   Regular, reflecting parts; rigid and measurable.

SYSTEM   A computer setup; short for Operating System.

T

TASTE   A preference.

TEMPLATE   A master document that can be used repeatedly without altering the original contents. Many applications provide templates or allow the use to create them. When opened they actually create a duplicate copy, which can be modified as needed and saved as a new file.

TERTIARY COLORS   Colors made of any mix of the three primaries (or two secondaries, or complementary colors); "brown" or chromatic neutrals.

TEXT TOOL   Another name for the I-beam pointer.

THRESHOLD   The point in vision at which an individual can just distinguish between two close samples.

TIFF   Acronym for Tag Image File Format, the standard file format for high-resolution bit-mapped graphics.

TINT   A pure color diluted, made lighter, or with white added.

TITLE BAR   The horizontal strip across the top of a window that contains its name. An active window has a title bar with horizontal stripes, a zoom box, and a close box.

TONE   A nonspecific word referring to change in value, light or dark, within a hue.

TRACKBALL   A device for moving the pointer on the screen. The trackball rolls in a stationary holder instead of sliding around on a pad, like a mouse.

TRACKPAD   A touch-sensitive pointing device built into late-model laptop computers. Instead of moving a pointer by rolling a trackball, a fingertip can be run across the trackpad.

TRANSITION   A change in steps or intervals from one form, color, size, surface, repeat, or other element to another.

TRANSPARENCE ILLUSION   An illusion in which opaque colors are made to appear transparent, done by overlapping two different colors and placing the middle mix of the two in the area of overlap.

TRASH   A desktop icon into which files are stored for later deletion.

TYPE   Originally "type" meant an actual block and raised letter that was inked for use in printing. It now means any character, letter, number, or mark.

TYPEFACE   A collection of letters, numbers, punctuation marks, and symbols with an identifiable and consistent design. A typeface can include many different weights (light, semibold, bold, outline, etc.) and styles (regular, italic, etc.).

U

UNCIAL A written hand that developed in the third century. An *uncial* is a Roman inch; its size became the name for the reed- or quill-written letters that evolved into small letters originally based on Roman (carved) capitals.

UPLOAD To send information from one's own computer to another, remote computer.

USER GROUP A group of people who get together to share help and advice about their computers and software.

USER INTERFACE The way a computer (or a program) interacts with the user. For example, a Mac's interface uses graphic elements—icons, windows, buttons, menus, dialog boxes—and is called a Graphical User Interface, or GUI.

V

VALUE Relative light and dark, with or without the presence of hue. High-value samples are light; low-value samples are dark.

VECTOR-BASED SOFTWARE Applications in which the images are drawn with lines that are redrawn so quickly that no flicker is seen, rather than images made of dots. See **pixel-based software.**

VEHICLE A liquid, paste, viscous, wax, chalk, or other substance into which pigments, dyes, or other colorants may be introduced to form a medium such as oil paint, textile dye, or crayon.

VIRTUAL MEMORY A strategy that expands the available memory by treating vacant space on a hard disk as if it were RAM.

VIRTUAL REALITY A computer-generated image of an environment, projected by a headset directly onto the retina of the eye.

VIRUS A program that replicates itself from one file or disk to another without the user's knowledge or consent. Viruses are spread through floppy disks, networks, and on-line services and can go undetected (unless the user has an anti-viral utility) until something goes wrong. Some viruses deliberately destroy data, and even those designed to be "benign" can cause crashes, slowdowns, and file corruption.

VOICE RECOGNITION The ability of a computer to interpret and execute spoken commands and even, with the right software, to take dictation.

VOID An empty space; nothingness. In three-dimensional design, a gap or opening in a solid.

VOLUME The measurable space occupied by a three-dimensional mass (solid). Also, the measurable space of an interior void within a solid.

W

WAVELENGTH A pulse of energy emitted by a light source at specific distances apart. In wavelengths of visible light (visible energy) each wavelength is perceived as a separate color.

WEBER-FECHNER PRINCIPLE A mathematical series in which intervals between numbers are geometric (1, 2, 4, 8, 16, 32, 64, 128, etc.) in progression, each step double the one before and half the one following. Weber-Fechner series are used to illustrate visual intervals, particularly intervals of value.

WIDTH The side-to-side (left-to-right or horizontal) dimension of a two- or three-dimensional figure. See also **length.**

WINDOW A rectangular frame on a screen that has a title bar and scroll bars. Disks and folders open into windows, and documents appear in windows when they are being worked on.

WINDOWS Microsoft software that adds a graphical user interface to PCs.

WORD A block or group of letters together that represent a spoken word. In speaking, a word is an audible sign or symbol. A compound of phonetics.

WORD PROCESSOR Software that alloys the user to enter, edit, and format text. It can also provide spell-checkers, outlining, tables, footnotes, tables of contents, and other features.

WORLD COORDINATE SPACE The mathematically plotted three-dimensional grid for drawing three-dimensional objects with horizontal (X), vertical (Y), and depth (Z) axes.

WWW The World Wide Web, a network that is a subset of the Internet.

WYSIWYG Acronym for What You See Is What You Get; or, the image you on the screen matches what prints onto paper (pixel-based software). Pronounced "wizzywig."

X

X, Y, AND Z The three axes of world coordinate space.

Z

ZOOM BOX A small box at the right end of the title bar in most active windows. Clicking on it expands the window to display all the contents; a second click restores the previous size and shape.

BIBLIOGRAPHY

Albers, Josef. *Interaction of Colors.* New Haven: Yale University Press, 1963.

Armstrong, Tim. *Colour Perception: A Practical Approach to Colour Theory.* Tarquin Publications: Norfolk, England, 1991.

Arnheim, Rudolf. *Art and Visual Perception.* Berkeley and Los Angeles: University of California Press, 1954.

———. *Visual Thinking.* Berkeley and Los Angeles: University of California Press, 1969.

Barrow, John D. *The Artful Universe.* England: Clarendon Press, undated.

Bartlett, John. *Familiar Quotations.* Boston: Little, Brown and Company, 1980.

Bates, John. *Basic Design.* Cleveland: World Publishing, 1960.

Billmeyer, Fred W., and Max Salzman. *Principles of Color Technology.* New York: Interscience Publishers, 1966.

Birren, Faber. *Color Perceptions in Art.* New York: Van Nostrand Reinhold, 1976.

———. *Color Psychology and Color Therapy.* New York: University Books, 1961.

———. *Color and Human Response,* New York: Van Nostrand Reinhold, 1978.

———. *Principles of Color.* West Chester, Pennsylvania: Schiffer Publishing Company, 1987.

Bowlt, John E., and Carol Washton-Long, eds. *The Life of Vassili Kandinsky: A Study On The Spiritual in Art.* Oriental Research Partners, 1980.

Canaday, John, ed. *Metropolitan Seminars in Art. Portfolio 6: Composition.* New York; Metropolitan Museum of Art, 1958.

Carter, Rob, Ben Day, and Philip Meggs. *Typographic Design: Form and Communication,* 2nd ed. New York: Van Nostrand Reinhold, 1993.

Carter, Thomas F. *The Invention of Printing in China and Its Spread Westward,* Rev. L.C. Goodrich. New York: The Ronald Press.

Chevreul, Michel Eugene. *The Principles of Harmony and Contrast of Colors and Their Applications to the Arts.* New York: Reinhold Publishing Company, 1967.

Ching, Francis D.K. *Building Construction Illustrated.* New York: Van Nostrand Reinhold Company Inc., 1975.

Ching, Francis D.K. *Architectural Graphics.* New York: Van Nostrand Reinhold Company Inc., 1975.

Cohen, Arthur, ed. *The New Art of Color: The Writings of Robert and Sonia Delaunay.* New York: The Viking Press, 1978.

Cotton, Bob and Richard Oliver. *The Cyberspace Lexicon.* London: Phaidon, 1994.

Crofton, Ian. *A Dictionary of Art.* London: Routledge, 1988.

Crozier, Ray. *Manufactured Pleasures—Psychological Responses to Design.* Manchester England: Manchester University Press, 1994.

Curtis, William Jr. *Le Corbusier: Ideas and Forms.* Oxford: England Phaidon Press Ltd., 1986.

De Grandis, Luigina. *Theory and Use of Colon,* trans. John Gilbert, New York: Harry N. Abrams Inc., Publishers, 1984.

Designer's Guide to Color. vol. I and II. Trans. James Stockton. San Francisco, California: Chronicle Books, 1984.

Diringer, David *The Alphabet.* London: Hutchinsons Scientific and Technical Publications, n.d.

Dreifus, Claudia. "The CyberMaxims of Esther Dysan." *New York Times.* July 7, 1996. Section 6, page 19.

Eiseman, Leatrice. *The PANTONE Book of Color.* New York: Harry N. Abrams, Publishers, 1990.

Esposito, Tony and Janet Post King. *Script Typeface Library,* vols. 1 and 2. New York: Van Nostrand Reinhold, 1994.

Evans, Ralph M. *An Introduction to Color.* New York: John Wiley and Sons, 1948.

Ferrini, Bruce P. *Medieval and Renaissance Illuminated Manuscripts,* catalogue 3. Akron, Ohio: Mitchell Graphics Inc., 1995.

————. *Important Western Medieval Illuminated Manuscripts and Illuminated Leaves,* catalogue 1. Akron, OH: Bruce P. Ferrini Rare Books, 1987.

Funk and Wagnalls. *Encarta* (CD-ROM). Microsoft® 1993–1995.

Geelhaar, Christian. *Paul Klee: Life and Work.* New York: Baron's Educational Series, 1982.

Goethe, Johann von Wolfgang. *Goethe's Color Theory,* trans. Rupprecht Matthei. New York: Van Nostrand Reinhold Company, 1971.

Goldstein, E. Bruce. *Sensation and Perception.* Belmont, California: Wadsworth Publishing Company, 1984.

Greenhalgh, Paul. *Quotations and Sources on Design and the Decorative Arts.* Manchester England: Manchester University Press, 1993.

Greiman, April. *Hybrid Imagery: The Fusion of Technology and Graphic Design.* London: Architecture Design and Technology Press, 1990.

Hale, Helen. *The Artist's Quotation Book.* London: Robert Hale, 1990.

Hoffman, Armin. *Graphic Design Manual, Principles and Practice.* New York: Van Nostrand Reinhold, 1965.

Hope, Augustine, and Margaret Walch. *The Color Compendium.* New York: Van Nostrand Reinhold Company, 1990.

Hoving, Thomas. *King of the Confessors.* New York: Ballantine Books, 1981.

The International Communications Foundation. *The Korean Language.* Seoul South Korea: Si-Sa-Yong-O-Sa Publishers Inc. and The International Communications Foundation, 1983.

Itten, Johannes. *The Elements of Color,* ed. Faber Birren; trans. Ernst Van Haagen. New York: Van Nostrand Reinhold Company, 1970.

————. *The Art of Color.* trans Ernst Van Haagen. New York: Van Nostrand Reinhold Company, 1961.

————. *The Basic Course at the Bauhaus,* rev. London: Thames and Hudson (also, Litton Educational Publishing), 1975.

Jenny, Peter. *The Sensual Fundamentals of Design.* Zurich, Switzerland: Verlag der Fachvereine, 1991.

Kandinsky, Wassily. *Point and Line to Plane.* New York: Dover Publications Inc., 1979.

Krech, R., S. Crutchfield, and N. Livison. *Elements of Psychology,* 2nd ed. New York: Alfred A Knopf, 1979.

Labuz, Ronald. *The Computer in Graphic Design: From Technology to Style.* New York: Van Nostrand Reinhold, 1993.

Lambert, Patricia. *Controlling Color.* New York: Design Press, 1991.

Larsen, Jack Lenor, and Jeanne Weeks. *Fabrics for Interiors.* New York: Van Nostrand Reinhold, 1975.

Lauer, David A., and Stephen Pentak. *Design Basics,* 4th ed. Fortworth: Harcourt Brace College Publishing Company, 1995.

Lewis, Peter H. "Apple's Best Hope: On-Line Sales." *New York Times.* August 13, 1996. Section C, page 5.

LeWitt, Sol. *Photo Grids.* New York: Paul David Press/Rizzoli, 1977.

Loveless, Richard, ed. *The Computer Revolution and the Arts.* Tampa: University of South Florida Press, 1986.

Luckiesh, M. *Visual Illusions: Their Characteristics and Applications.* New York: Dover Publications, Inc., 1965.

Lupton, Ellen, and J. Abbott Miller, eds. *The Bauhaus and Design Theory.* London: Thames and Hudson, 1993.

Mahnke, Frank H., and Rudolf H. Mahnke. *Color in Man Made Environments.* New York: Van Nostrand Reinhold, 1982.

Maier, Manfred. *Basic Principles of Design.* New York: Reinhold Company, Inc., 1980.

Makorny, Ulrike Becks. *Kandinsky.* Koln Germany: Benedikt Taschen, 1994.

Matsui, Keizo. *Three Dimensional Graphics.* Tokyo: Rikuyo-Sha, 1987.

Mayer, Ralph. *The Artist's Handbook of Materials and Techniques.* New York: The Viking Press, 1981.

McClelland, Deke. *Mastering Adobe Illustrator.* Home Wood, IL: Business One Irwin Desktop Publishing Library, 1991.

Munsell, Albert Henry. *A Grammar of Colors.* New York: Van Nostrand Reinhold, 1969.

Nesbitt, Alexander. *The History and Technique of Lettering.* New York: Dover Publications, Inc., 1957.

Nicolson, Marjorie Hope. *Newton Demands the Muse.* Princeton, New Jersey: Princeton University Press, 1966.

Ostwald, Wilhelm. *The Color Primer.* New York: Van Nostrand Reinhold, 1969.

Panero, Julius, and Martin Zelnik. *Human Dimensions and Interior Space.* New York: Whitney Library of Design, 1979.

Parsons, Thomas and Sons. *Historical Colours.* London: Thomas Parsons and Sons, 1934.

Pile, John. *Perspective for Interior Designers.* New York: Whitney Library of Design—Watson Guptil Publications, 1985.

Poore, Henry R. *Art Principles in Practice.* New York: G.P. Putnam's Sons/The Knickerbocker Press, 1930.

Potter, Norman. *What is A Designer?* London/New York: Studio-Vista (Van Nostrand Reinhold), 1960.

Roman, Klara G. *Encyclopedia of the Written Word.* New York: F. Ungar, 1968.

Rood, Ogden. *Modern Chromatics.* New York: Van Nostrand Reinhold, 1973.

Sargent, Walter. *The Enjoyment and Use of Color.* New York: Dover Publications, Inc., 1964.

Scott, Robert Gilliam. *Design Fundamentals.* New York: McGraw Hill Book Company, Inc., 1951.

Shlain, Leonard. *Art and Physics: Parallel Visions in Space, Time and Light.* New York: William Morrow Inc., 1991.

Sloane, Patricia. *The Visual Nature of Color.* New York: Design Press, 1989.

Solso, Robert L. *Cognition and the Visual Arts.* Cambridge, Massachusettes: the MIT Press, 1994.

Tanaka, Ikko. *Japan Color.* San Francisco: Chronicle Books, 1982.

Taylor, Joshua C. *Learning to Look.* Chicago: University of Chicago Press, 1927.

Theroux, Alexander. *The Primary Colors.* New York: Henry Holt and Company, 1994.

Tufte, Edward R. *Envisioning Information.* Cheshire, Connecticut Graphics Press, 1990.

UNESCO. *The Art of Writing.* Paris, France: UNESCO, 1965.

Venturi, Lionello. *History of Art Criticism.* New York: E.P. Dutton and Co., 1964.

Vince, John. *The Language of Computer Graphics.* London: Architecture Design and Technology Press, 1990.

Walch, Margaret. *Color Source Book.* New York: Scribner, 1979.

Washburn, Dorothy, and Donald Crow. *Symmetries of Culture Theory and Practice of Plane Pattern Analysis.* Seattle: University of Washington Press, 1988.

Webster's New Twentieth Century Dictionary Unabridged, 2nd ed.

Wolchonek, Louis. *The Art of Three-Dimensional Design.* New York: Dover, 1959.

———. *Design for Artists and Craftsmen.* New York: Dover, 1953.

Wolff, Henry. *Visual Thinking: Methods for Making Images Memorable.* New York: American Showcase Inc., 1988.

Wolfflin, Heinrich. *Classic Art.* New York: Phaidon Publishers Inc., Oxford University Press, 1952.

Wong, Wucious. *Principles of Two Dimensional Design.* New York: Van Nostrand Reinhold Company, 1972.

Zuckerman, Laurence. "The Designer Who Made the Mac Smile." *New York Times.* August 26, 1996. Section D, p. 5.

ILLUSTRATIONS

PAGES: 3, 18, 19, 21, 23, 25, 39, 41, 42, 44, 45, 47, 49, 51, 59, 66, 73, 77, 83, 84, 91, 93, 103, 105, 106, 108, 109, 112, 123, 127, 129, 132, 146, 148, 149, 150, 153-164, Color Plates, 2, 3, 4, 6, 7, 9, 10, 11, 13, 14, 15, 16, 17, 19 Ed Noriega

Cover Credit: Alinari/Art Resource NY, Cupola, Medici Chapel, S. Lorenzo, Florence, Italy. Illustrations by Ed Noriega.

COLOR PLATES:

1	Schalkwijk/Art Resource NY
5	Esteban Vicente
8	Lydia Johnston
12	Ad. et M. P. Verneuil collection of Linda Holtzschue
18	Jany Tran

INDEX